Roll Back the Years
'The way we were'

Aspects of life in the Ring of Gullion in the 1940s and 50s

D1826114

Hugh A Murphy

SHANWAY PRESS

Copyright © 2024 Hugh A Murphy

ISBN 978-1-910044-60-5

Shanway Press
15 Crumlin Road
Belfast
www.shanway.com

*Including an anthology of unpublished work and
extensive collection of poems*

Acknowledgements

I want to thank my brother, Joe Murphy, and his son, Cathal, for the valuable assistance they gave in assembling this material.

I am indebted to my son, Mario Murphy, in undertaking the onerous task of steering this material towards publication.

As always, I am grateful to my daughter, Sharon Mc Kenna, for acting once more here as my unpaid promoter.

A very special thank you goes to Eamonn Mallie for the large amount of work he did on my behalf; I have in mind particularly the recitals that he organised, both in public and online, of many of the poems included here.

Foreword

Hugh, as my Irish and Latin teacher I always affectionately called you 'Aodh Dubh'. I'd be lying if I neglected to say some of my fellow pupils had other names for you! Sir, we all respected you from the day you walked into our class and declared, 'Latinam nunc habemus'. I felt at home in your class, as a child of 'a hedge school' from the foot of Slieve Gullion. You were 'a hard man' but you didn't intimidate 'a boy' like me from Silverbridge who saw Mullaghbawn off the pitch time after time!

You inspired me and deepened my passion for languages especially for Irish. You left me with an insatiable appetite for new phrases, poetry and literature.

You were not alone in making such a contribution to my education. It is quite remarkable to think that you, Tommy Keane and Patsy Rice who were reared within a stone's throw of each other would have such an impact on my life. South Armagh abú!

My brother Michael who worked in the Science labs. in the Abbey shared an anecdote with me involving the late Joe Devlin from Cullyhannna. He told me each morning on walking into the staff room Joe asked you the same question, 'How are they all on the side of the hill this morning?'. If this was meant to be something of a put-down by Joe, Hugh I say 'didn't we all do ok from the 'side of the hill?''.

You were more than a language teacher Hugh, you were a philosopher. Tommy Fegan who was another of your pupils in our class reminded me of the day you looked out through the window of the classroom and said 'Do you see that tree? It talks to me and I talk to it.' Tommy assures me he hasn't stopped talking to trees since! That step outside the curriculum didn't stop there. I vividly recall the day you looked at raindrops on a pane of glass on the outside of the window and you asked us, 'Have you any idea how far that raindrop might have travelled to land up on that window? Every day it rains I am reminded of that profound question which you posed Sir. And there was more Hugh. In another exposition you dramatically raised the testosterone levels in us young innocent males of fifteen and sixteen years when you declared, 'It is only when you examine the bone structure of the female form that you can really appreciate the beauty in woman'. I can only conclude your observation was informed by your beautiful wife Mary. Go ndéana Dia trócaire ar Mháire.

The greatest compliment I can pay to you Hugh is by continuing to bring your wonderful poetry to a wider audience and I pledge to you I will do that.

Despite my modesty (which ought to forbid me putting this in writing), I will conclude with this kind remark which you often made about me in the presence of my peers in Abbey CBS. You said, 'in years to come out there in South Armagh they'll be saying, "Sin an fear a raibh aigne chinn aige".

Go raibh maith agat Aoidh. Go Maire tú ibhfad.

Le meas..

Eamonn Mallie.

Contents

Introduction

The Ring of Gullion is an ancient place. It still bears the hallmarks of its distant past, not least in its name. For this we must go back more than sixty million years to a time when Slieve Gullion and the area immediately surrounding it was covered by a large volcanic dome, the result of persistent eruptions over an extended period. At the end of the last ice age glaciers moved down south eastwards through the dome, gouging out two valleys, one to the east and one to the west of Slieve Gullion. The hard basalt core of the mountain itself remained immovable. Today it acts as the hub of a circle of low hills and mountains which surround it. These are the remnants of the original dome.

If we jump forward many years to the dawn of the historical period, we see the mountain playing host to a number of myths and legends. These deal almost exclusively with CuChulainn and Fionn Mac Cumhaill and give us a clear insight into aspects of their supposed lives.

If we move from there to the seventeenth century, the period of greatest change in Ireland, we come to the era of St. Oliver Plunkett and Bishop Patrick Donnelly. Oliver Plunkett came to Ireland as Primate in the year 1670. He very soon had to go into hiding in the vastness of Slieve Gullion. On one occasion he was marooned in the southern cairn for a period of three months when the pursuit was at its height. During that period his needs were catered for by James McKenna his servant.

He was finally captured, tried and found guilty on false evidence supplied by men from South Armagh. Bishop Patrick Donnelly was a pupil of St. Oliver and was ordained to the priesthood by him. By and large he had a more fortunate time in the Ring of Gullion than St. Oliver. In all he remained there for forty six years in a number of different roles including that of Primate.

During our youth in the Ring of Gullion we did not think that we were in any way special. It is only now with the benefit of hindsight that it is clear that we were. We were standing on the outer edge of a lifestyle that had remained permanent down through the centuries but was about to disappear virtually overnight. With it would go the traditions which had formed the backbone of Irish rural society, the communal harvesting, the fairs, the trashing, the céilí house, and numerous others. We were the last generation that would be able to avail of them.

I leave here an echo of those traditions so that future generations may gain some idea of the way we were.

The Infant school

The first thing to exercise our minds was school. When my turn came to make the journey in 1945 I had not far to travel, merely across the road. I had long envied the older children who passed each day looking so important with their schoolbags on their backs and I could scarcely wait to join them.

The day at last came and I headed off across the road to Lislea School, the new leather satchel tightly fixed, with its single jotter and pencil. The teacher, Mrs. Donaghy, put me sitting in the front seat beside her and generally made a great fuss of me. Before the day was out I had taken my first step to paradise when she presented me with a new hard-backed book, which contained all the knowledge that there was in the world! I remember clutching it in my hand in triumph that evening on my way home, my badge of learning much too important to be hidden in a schoolbag!

The infants' room was quite sparse. As you came through the main door, before you entered the classroom, there was a small porch with a row of hooks for hanging up coats along the back wall. On a wet morning there would be pools of water on the floor as all pupils walked to school at that time, and some of them quite a distance.

Inside there were four rows of desks down just over half the length of the room, with a large table for the teacher at the top. To the left of this was a blackboard resting on an easel. There was no such thing as central heating or lighting at that time, anywhere in Lislea. The heating in the classroom was provided by a large, free-standing "barrel" stove from which a round asbestos chimney led up through the ceiling. During winter on cold or wet days we were all allowed to gather in a circle around the stove. It produced a great amount of heat. When the fire was at its height the outside would glow red.

During writing practice, after we had mastered a sufficient amount of the alphabet, "writing slates" were handed out. These were about the size of an A4 page and we practiced copying the letters on them with chalk. When the exercise was over we would clean them with cloths that were supplied and they would be collected again and left on the teacher's table.

There was a short break each day at half ten, the "free milk break". The milk would be delivered each morning and the crates stored at the back of the room. The milk came in small, squat bottles with a flanged top. Inserted in this was a flat cardboard stopper with a small perforated circle in its centre. Each pupil pushed this inwards and inserted a drinking straw from a box which stood beside the crates. This was always a welcome break.

My initial impression of Mrs Donaghy on my first day at school was to remain unchanged throughout my "infant education", a kind, protective person, almost a mother-like figure, with a warmth that was close to affection.

The only time I ever saw her in any way flustered was on the much feared day of the ecclesiastical inspection when her true merit as a teacher was being assessed by the powers almighty on the basis of how well she had instilled into us the time-honoured, unquestioned ritual of the catechism.

I remember especially an occasion when the older children, including my sister Ann and my brother Joe, were being examined for Confirmation and I found myself, unwittingly, the focus of attention for a brief period. Many weeks of preparation had preceded the event, with much chanting and individual reciting of answers filling our ears from the right hand side of the room where the intended victims were gathered, as we "worked on" in the middle rows.

When the great day arrived and the usual questioning and "spontaneous" answering was in full flight the priest suddenly departed from his brief and asked if anyone knew where St. Brigid was buried. When there seemed to be a silence and no one replying I put up my hand, much to the bemusement of both priest and teacher and informed him that she was buried in Downpatrick along with St.Patrick and St. Colmcill. I have no idea where I had got this information from but it was knowledge I assumed everyone had and of no great importance. However it seemed to invoke a certain amount of interest in the ecclesiastical inspector. He came over to me and started to ask other questions from the Confirmation list, and naturally, I, like all the other victims who had been on the receiving end of the constant chanting from beyond for weeks previously, knew them off by heart.

After some whispered conferring with Mrs. Donaghy the inspector announced solemnly that I was "ready" and should join the others. For a brief period I felt like a hero, but that only lasted until I got home and my mother R.I.P. discovered that she had not only two children to kit out for Confirmation but three! The general feeling was that I should have "kept my big mouth shut".

Although those infant days with Mrs Donaghy were happy ones, the euphoria I felt on that first day at school gradually wore off, as it eventually dawned on me that this "school-going" was to be a permanent condition and that it had many disadvantages, especially the curtailment of the unlimited freedom that I had had in the previous years. I longed for the weekend, or at least for the evening, when I could again be free.

My most frequent excursion, as often as discretion would allow, was out to the toilet which was situated on the left hand side below the main door, against the graveyard wall. There was a large stone beside the toilet, adjacent to the perimeter wall of the yard along the road. When I stood on the top of this stone my eyes were just about level with the top of the wall. From there I could look through the parallel stones on the top and see our house, and the journey from where I was to it seemed forever, and the time between me and escape was eternity!

Throughout the rest of my life, until it was finally removed during later renovations of the old school, that stone was to remain for me a symbol of imprisonment. What first fixed that image in my mind was an occasion early in my school life when I stood on the stone one morning and watched my father driving the cattle out from the byre on to the road on his way with them to Donnelly's hill.

As my father reached the road he stopped to light his pipe and as the first smoke rose and mingled with the steam still rising from the cows' flanks it was like an image from Heaven, the ultimate symbol of unfettered freedom.

INCARCERATION

I stood on the grey stone,
My gaze skewered
On the gapped ridge of the wall,
A prisoner to the schoolyard,
As my father drove the cattle out.

The dull thud of hooves called
The smell of the byre
Rising from flanks
The close warmth of the straw,
And my father's pipe spoke
In the cold air
As they melted away to Donnelly's hill,
Their freedom bolting my cage.

Every time I see the stone
I remember
Twenty years of cells.
Nothing can be as free
As my father's image
That morning
As he walked away from me
Forever
Into the stillness of the morning air.

The Senior School

When I moved into the senior classroom life was quite different to the more relaxed atmosphere of the infants' room. We were dealing now with serious learning and a much more formal regime applied, where a quick mind, or at least a quick wit, was a useful tool for survival. We had learned the basic principles of letters and numbers in the infants' class but we soon found out that there was much more to this than "one and one makes two" and "the cat sat on the mat". We were now in a new world where reading had to be done from large books with continuous paragraphs and where mathematics moved into the advanced stages of unheard of concepts such as multiplication, subtraction, and even long division.

These latter nightmares were contained in a harmless looking, hard backed, book which we always carried with us and to which the master alone held the key, "The Answer Book." Many hours were spent at night, with the help of my mother, working out these imponderables. Having the right answer, however, was no guarantee of safety, unless your answer happened to correspond with the one in the "The Answer Book". If not swift retribution was normally exacted on the spot. This book, although we soon came to suspect its infallibility, was always inviolate and never subject to appeal.

The master's table was placed across the room at the upper gable wall, and to the right of this, as you came in through the main door, was a row of display cabinets, the first of which contained an array of stuffed animals. I remember especially a fox with head turned looking straight at you as if you had just interrupted him momentarily as he passed. There was also a badger, a squirrel, and a number of smaller animals and an impressive selection of birds, especially a pheasant which never failed to hold my attention. There were also sand-filled trays of birds' eggs of different sizes and colours. Next to this was a display which always fascinated me, a host of multifarious shaped bottles and phials which contained various coloured granules and liquids. Their mystery was added to by the fact that they always remained out of reach as the cabinets were never opened and we knew instinctively that even the remotest interference with them would be followed by instant execution.

In front of the table there was an open space, between it and the start of the rows of desks which ran with precision in arrow-straight lines to the back of the room where a door opened on the left wall into the infants' room. In the middle of this space stood the blackboard, resting on an easel. This was the gathering area where we assembled at various times each day with bated breath for individual reading practice, and also for arithmetic. Any shortcomings were immediately apparent and were dealt with severely. Many a victim was sent out to cut the instrument of his own execution from the hedge along the road.

Writing practice consisted of a headline, which the master put on the board in beautiful copperplate writing, and which we had to copy down through a full page of our exercise books. All writing was done with ink pens, long narrow wooden shafts with a nib attached. Each desk was supplied with an inkwell, which was always kept topped up, and a supply of blotting paper.

There was always a sense of urgency to get the copying finished so that we would have time to "herd the sheep". These were small white insects which always seemed to be in plentiful supply in the old wooden desks, especially in the cup beneath the inkwell. We soon found out that they had an aversion to ink. The competition was to gather as many of them together onto your desk as you could find, normally by letting them crawl up a piece of paper, and then "herd" them by putting a circle of ink around them. Many an hour was spent by those of us lucky enough to sit in the desks towards the back of the class "herding our sheep" rather than honing our minds.

The Inspector

One of the most feared visitors to the school in those days was the inspector. Unlike today his arrival was not normally signalled in advance, except on the rare occasion when the word spread along the "grapevine" that an inspector was doing the rounds in the area.

On such occasions we all immediately went into action stations. The room was cleaned from top to bottom, the lines of desks were plumbed, unpresentable pages were neatly removed from exercise books and special pieces of reading were prepared for fluid delivery on the big day.

These occasions, however, were all too rare and the inspector's visits were almost always unheralded, and planned with a considerable degree of care and, I might say, cunning, by the inspector so as to create as large an element of surprise as possible. I remember one such occasion especially, during one of the lazier days of summer, as the master relaxed after lunch in his armchair with the newspaper held out before him as usual and we, thankful for this daily period of respite, relaxed peacefully in our desks.

The first indication we had of impending disaster was the soft tingle of finger touching latch in the hall porch. The inspector, a thin-faced, wiry man with a narrow, elongated head, surmounted with a thinning crop of greying hair, who would remind you for all the world of an inverted exclamation mark, bounced into the room. He had, as usual, parked his car, an Austin 7, up the road behind our house and had come down furtively, un-noticed by anyone, along the hedge and in past the girls' toilet.

I still remember vividly, and with a great sense of admiration, that single, fluid, all-in-one reaction of the master as both hands came together instantly in a circular movement whipping the paper into a ball and straight into the bin, and a pen appeared magically in his hand writing casually on the notepad before him. He raised his head slowly with mild curiosity at this unexpected, but quite obviously welcome, interruption to his daily grind as the inspector's feet landed on the floor and the look of triumph gradually faded from his face.

Asking Out

One of the greatest occasions for any of us was the odd glorious day when our services were required at home and we would be told to "ask out", indicating clearly to the master that this was at our parents' request. There was never a question, at least in our case, of our parents keeping us at home on their own initiative, without this ritual being adhered to. This was at a time when the schoolmaster's position was almost sacred, second only in importance to the Parish Priest. I remember such a day, not long after I had been promoted to the senior room, when potatoes were being set in the field behind our house. After much persuasion during the course of the weekend I had managed to convince my father that my services would be indispensable on the Monday morning to drop the seed, and I finally got the nod "to ask out."

I still remember the sense of trepidation as I got up from the seat shortly after the roll was called and began to walk up the floor towards the master's table, something that was never done on a normal day unless you were summoned. His sense of surprise and slightly deprecating smile did not help my confidence as I choked out my request.

"Dropping seed? Sure you wouldn't be fit to drop seed!" And then after an eternity those glorious words, "Go ahead!"

I can still remember that feeling of total exhilaration as my feet landed on the road, still shaking with disbelief that I was actually free. The irony of it was missed on me then, just as it was missed on the large number of those I remember kicking their schoolbag up the road before them on their last day at school, and who the next day might well be seen out in the fields covered with muck digging shores with the rain running down their neck. Free, but free for a day's drudgery, dropping seed, one of the most backbreaking jobs in the annual cycle of tasks. But that didn't matter then. I was out!

THE SETTING

The drills lined the field
Ruler-straight,
The neat margin of siderigs
Blotted with heaps of seed
Freshly cut,
Wet tongues licking the sun.
My legs gulped the road
Up the school-hill
Hands still shaking, his gruff consent
Unbelieved in my ears,
And my father's ready smile,
"So he let you out! Here's the knife.
Mind you make it tight.
Cut the neck wide."
And he turned, graip in hand,
Shooting the dung with expert flick
Down the drill, my mother watching
From the gap, proud in his strength.
The apron stung my neck, gouged my legs
As I walked performing the ritual,
The full udder of seed milked slow
In the cable-drill, pulling me on,
Breaking my back, chained
To an instinct as inhuman as his
For the satisfaction to stand at the day's end
Consumed by the wide expanse
Of a spud-field
Hatching his dream.

Election Day

The most welcome event, undoubtedly, during our early days in Lislea school had nothing at all to do with academia, and it was one that we felt happened all too seldom, election day!

The school was always used at that time as a Polling Station. This meant not only a day off, but also the prospect of an occasion of colour and pageant, with banners and placards and general commotion. This was the only time that we saw cars gathered together in any numbers in Lislea, as each available vehicle in the area was commissioned to ferry the aged and infirm from all parts and the able-bodied from outlying regions. This was at a time, in the late 1940's, when the fortunes of the Nationalist Party were on the up and there was a great sense of excitement and urgency as every effort was made to ensure that no vote was left unclaimed.

The actual voting took place in the senior room on the right, but the infants' room on the left was also a hive of activity. During these times we as children always referred to this room, with a complete sense of innocence I must add, as "The Changing Room." And this was exactly what it was.

It was here that the women gathered often throughout the course of the day and various items of apparel were exchanged, rain-coats, fur-coats, fox and mink stoles, hats, glasses, shoes, and anything else that was removable, in endless combinations which produced multifarious guises that ensured that every potential voter was represented. The fact that a number of them were sleeping peacefully in Lislea graveyard was a matter of little moment.

The Master always acted as Presiding Officer on these occasions, standing like a statesman inside the main door, nodding in sage recognition to each of the hybrids as they passed.

I remember on one occasion my mother getting an urgent call a few minutes before the poll closed. Her mild protestations that she had already voted eight times that day were brushed aside. She was informed that there had been a slight miscount and that Mrs. Crossan's R.I.P. vote had not yet been "called in". And, so, a quick sally to the Polls and another vote was won!

Honour

The most graphic of all my memories from my early days at Lislea school was the morning that I stood outside my father's house in fascinated awe as a local pupil, and a personal friend of mine, was marched to school with grim-faced determination by his father on a horse's halter.

The pupil, the dearest soul I have ever known, had apparently absconded from school one spring morning into the freedom of hills and fields. This was at a time when "mitching", unlike today, was still taboo and carried with it a great family stigma. When the father found out, he determined to exact an extreme and public retribution, sufficient in its severity to ensure that family honour was saved.

I still remember the image that morning as both of them marched down the centre of the road, the young lad in front with his father walking resolutely behind at a distance of the full extension of two twenty-foot horse reins, one held firmly in each hand, just like a man ploughing. The other ends of the reins were looped in a halter around the lad's head. Thus, he had marched him the long distance from home and delivered him up to the master at the school door.

That image burned itself into my brain that day and has never left me. It has raised questions in my mind often about people's reactions, including my own, to various situations where our responses are dictated more by prevailing conventions and codes than by reason.

The poignancy of this scene was given an added edge which made it almost tragic a short number of years later when whatever chance that lad had of any freedom in his life was terminated forever when he was blown to pieces at work during blasting operations, his hard-won education virtually untouched.

I was attending University at the time in Belfast, sitting as usual in the evening listening to the six o' clock news as I took my tea, when the words that I had just heard gradually sank in.

EXPLOSION

I remember the day in Belfast
The cultivated voice
Honing the name from the box.
How unusual to hear "Lislea"
From a radio station in London.
The blast ripped him apart
The gelignite erect for his shovel,
Orgasm of death.
And I had seen him at mass
The previous Sunday.

His mother stood at the door
Protesting
To the parish priest and the copper,
In conspiracy of truth Unnatural.
"Pete's not dead
His tea is ready.
He left me a note
On the table this morning,
Look!
Propped up by the jug –
Pete's living!"

The original scene that morning came back to haunt me many years later when I was back living at home. On hearing a strange noise outside, I went to the window and looked out and found the image being virtually replicated before my eyes. There coming down the centre of the road was a local farmer, walking at the full extent of the reins, one held tightly in each hand, holding back firmly against the pull of a haltered bullock straining his way in front. It was being led, in its mad, forward dash of urgency, on the first phase of its journey from the upland farm to Camlough fair and thence to the meat factory and the slaughter.

AN ECHO

I remember him pulled along on a chaffed halter,
Taut against shame,
Ready to explode for the nearest ditch
Into the ecstasy of fields, unshuttered learning,
His father sombre-faced in his dedication,
Haltering him along to the master.
Wild innocence on a short fuse
Detonated at the corner, the gelignite
Punctuating his learning.

But still the face hovers, transparent,
To be filled often, like now
When the farmer passes
Back straight against the pull
The bullock beating harsh syllables,
On the drummed road.
Staccato for the slaughter.

The Annual Play

The only cultural event in Lislea during my early years was the annual play staged by Lislea Dramatic Players. This was an occasion much anticipated by us, and one that always gave rise to much discussion. All that we would have would be the name of the play — The Playboy of the Western World; Mungo's Mansion; The Plough and the Stars; Riders to the sea etc. — but that was sufficient to whet our appetite. As the weeks turned to days the level of excitement grew, until eventually the great night arrived. It is difficult to describe the feeling as we at last headed down the road in the dark with the entrance money clutched in our hand towards Lislea Hall, a tin structure situated along the main road just below the Chapel. The nearest would be the magic of Christmas Night when the waiting was at last over and the great man himself was about to arrive.

As I entered the hall I was always struck by the special aroma associated with the place, a smell of antiquity, warmth, mystique. Wooden foldaway chairs were laid out in two wide rows the full length of the hall, with a passageway left in the centre and along both sides. This added to the sense of size, which to us seemed enormous. Along both walls were oil lamps turned up full which made the hall quite bright and caused the waxed floor between the chairs to glisten.

Along the front of the stage were the footlights, again a row of oil lamps which were concealed on the audience side by a wooden V-shaped canopy, the inside of which was backed with tin to throw the light outwards onto the stage. Along the front of the hall closest to the stage were two rows of forms for the young people. It was on these that we sat, with an unimpeded view of the stage. From behind the curtain strange noises would always be emanating, the sound of sawing, hammering, and objects being dragged across the stage, as the seats in the hall gradually filled up. These noises added to the sense of mystery and it was all that we could do to resist moving across the short distance from the forms and peeping behind the curtain. However, we knew that such an act was completely taboo in Lislea hall and that the penalty would be instant death! Eventually the noises would begin to die down until they gradually ceased. By this time the hall would be filled to capacity. This was an event in Lislea that no one ever missed, including a number from outside.

Finally, after what seemed an eternity, the great moment would arrive. The producer, Terry O'Hanlon, would put his head out through the curtain, only his head, with the curtain held tightly beneath his chin lest anyone might get even a glimpse of what lay beyond, and announce the magic words, "Would Mickey O'Neill put out the lights, please."

Mickey would duly get up with a small stool in his hand and proceed from the top right-hand corner of the hall to extinguish the lights one by one. As he moved on his excruciatingly slow course around the hall an eclipsing darkness followed him and the sense of mystery, excitement, and anticipation closed in ever tighter. Eventually the hall would be in total darkness, the only lights left being the footlights, casting a shimmering glow on the curtains. Gradually these would begin to move slowly sideways, revealing piece by piece the magical world that lay beyond.

We always identified completely with the characters in the play and with the evolving plot. For me it became completely real and the actors assumed the status of heroic figures. Although these were people whom I knew well, and many of whom I saw daily, they were transformed completely on stage as I was drawn deeper and deeper into the plot. It might be twenty minutes into the play before I realised that the old man sitting in the corner was Pat Hannaway, or that the unkempt beggar was Francis Mc Parland, my own uncle, and that the angry man with the stick was Brian Mc Cann. The sorrow of Pegeen Mike as the image of her heroic playboy disintegrates before her eyes, or Captain Boyle and Joxer sitting on an empty stage gazing at the stars, or the tragedy of the corpse carried in from the sea wrapped in a tarpaulin and laid out on the table were real, living events.

The thing that fascinated me most was the magic of the words, the way they could create and define the characters and weave the story, with joy, sorrow, love, or tragedy emanating from them. The thought of one day being able to send words dancing across a stage, or lilting down a page, filled me with awe and longing.

When the play would be over I always felt a sense of anti-climax when the actors moved out from behind the stage to mingle with the audience. It seemed much too soon for them to come back to the blood and flesh of reality. I would have much preferred for them to remain in the world which they had created for us. However, they were raised in my esteem, and would be for many weeks. They were the sowers of deep-planted seed, the heroes of the hour, and the heroes of my days.

A New Era

During the 1940s, and for a period after, the landscape of Lislea and the surrounding area was a patchwork of small farms, worked by the horse. These farms had been handed down from father to son for generations and were the only form of existence the people had. Virtually all the lads who left Lislea School at 14, the then leaving age, went straight on to the farm.

Each small farmer owned one horse, which was sufficient for most of the work throughout the year, except in springtime. For ploughing and drilling two horses were required. For this purpose each farmer had a "join", either a neighbour or a family friend.

Each spring their two horses were put together as a team and the work was done consecutively on each farm. Most farmers kept their horse for three or four seasons and then replaced it. This was always a fairly anxious time and involved much discussion. Having a good horse was always of paramount importance, and also a source of a certain amount of pride. It was essential that the replacement would be, if possible, better than the one being exchanged, but this depended on a very discerning eye and also a certain amount of luck. It was not unknown for a degree of trickery to be employed in the horse fair in Camlough, especially by dealers, to alter one's impression of an animal. For example, a lazy, lethargic horse could be transformed utterly with a shot of ginger under the tail which caused him to sparkle with unbridled energy and spirit. The unsuspecting buyer would not be aware of this until the effect of the ginger wore off, normally by the time he was arriving home.

My own father, who was a fairly shrewd judge of a horse, was caught out himself on at least two occasions. The first was when he ended up with a very nice mare that was a great worker, provided you kept her on the straight. As soon as you asked her to make a turn she would stumble and fall. She had a fairly well concealed form of head-staggers. As a result, as soon as she reached the headrig or the footrig where a turn had to be made my uncle, the man with whom my father was joined, would have to run forward and catch her by the tail and keep her upright until the turn was made.

On the second occasion my father had a fine young horse that was perfect in every aspect of work until, as he grew older, he took to exploring the countryside. Eventually, no matter what field you would put him into, he would soar across even the highest ditch and away. We called him the jumper. Finally, and with great reluctance, my father had to get rid of him.

Some years later when another exchange was being made my father arrived home with a beautiful horse. He was almost sixteen hands high, with a sleek coat and rippling muscles. My father was very proud of his conquest. As we all stood around examining him my mother said that for some reason, which she couldn't quite put her finger on, he seemed vaguely familiar. He was finally let loose into the field below the house and we all watched in admiration as he went galloping around the field kicking his hind legs in the air, as horses do when released into a new paddock. When he reached the bottom of the field where there was a high ditch with a wide shuck behind it, without even slackening pace, he took off and soared as graceful as a swan over ditch and shuck with yards to spare and went off galloping up through Donnelly's land. The jumper was back!

At that time I was still attending Lislea National School, just across the road from my father's house and each day I came home at dinnertime to get my lunch. One day in the spring of 1947 as I crossed the road as usual a sight met my eyes that stopped me in my tracks. There in the yard in front of the stable door was a brand new tractor, with a new two-score plough attached to it!

I went up to the wonder almost holding my breath and looked in fascination at the shining bonnet, the twin wing mirrors stretching out to the right and left, the horn with the round rubber ball at the end, and the massive back tyres with the large rubber grips which were as deep as my hand. I walked around it again and again, noting the make, Ferguson, stamped in large letters on a plaque on the front of the bonnet, and the number-plate, LZ1944. I had never been this close to a tractor before. There were only two others in adjoining town lands, one in Ballinaleck and one in Levelamore. This was the first one ever in Lislea.

When I went inside I found that the tractor had been delivered to my father that morning from Hosford's, the tractor dealer in Newry. The man who had driven it out was still there eating his dinner. Part of the contract was that he would stay for one day to instruct my father in the operation of the new machinery.

The rest of that day at school seemed like a week. When I was finally released I gulped down my dinner and set off running up the road to Boyle's field where the tractor was working. My father was coming down the field ploughing, his two hands clutching either side of the steering wheel as though he were holding the ends of a pair of reins. The "tutor" was standing on the back of the tractor issuing instructions.

I sat on the bottom ditch of the field watching in fascination as the twin scores flowed out from behind the plough, up and down the field, at a speed which, in comparison to a pair of horses and a single score plough, seemed unreal. After a while the tutor came and joined me on the ditch and lit a cigarette. My father worked on now on his own, apparently fully qualified.

That evening after tea and before the Hosford man left there was still one more task to do, to get the tractor into the stable. The whole family came out in the dusk, including my mother, and everyone shouted directions as my father reversed slowly in through the twin doors – "a bit more to the left – watch out on your right! – back away – back away – Whoa! Whoa!

The tractor was finally stabled, with just a couple of inches to spare on either side, the twin tracks of the large back tyres clearly visible across the floor in the thin film of dried manure that still lay on the surface. The twin doors were closed and barred. A new era had begun.

Harvesting

A great deal of the jobs on the small farms during my childhood and youth were communal affairs. This applied especially to the corn cutting and the thrashing.

The only reapers that were available at that time were "drag reapers". These were pulled behind the horse, or in our case after 1947 the tractor. The cutting knife was operated by the motion of the reaper's wheels. After we acquired the tractor my father adapted the horse reaper by cutting off the two long shafts and attaching a drawbar to the centre so that it could be pulled by the tractor.

The only way of cutting the crops prior to the reaper was with the scythe. This was a much slower and much more arduous method. However, the day of the scythe was by no means over. You could not just pull into a field with a drag reaper and start cutting. A pathway had to be made for it first. This was done by cutting a wide swathe with the scythe the whole way around the field and, in addition, large turning areas at the two bottom corners.

During the corn cutting either my brother Joe or myself, as soon as my feet could reach the pedals, would drive the tractor while my father sat on the reaper seat "shaving". The latter was quite a risky task as the nature of the "shaver's" job meant that he was always leaning over the track of the cutting knife. For cutting any crop, either hay or corn that required to be gathered up and tied in sheaves a wooden tailboard would be fitted to the back of the cutting bar which housed the knife. From this board a stirrup extended upwards on the left hand side in front of the reaper seat. When pressed forward by foot the back of the tailboard would rise up off the ground; when released the tailboard would fall back flat again.

The shaver had a special "shaving rake". This was quite different to a normal rake. It consisted of a fairly thick base, slightly less in width than that of the tailboard, with a row of wooden teeth extending directly downwards. The handle was set at an angle so that when the rake was lowered it fell exactly level along the width of the tailboard.

When the reaper was in motion the shaver would press the stirrup forward raising the back of the tailboard until he judged that sufficient corn, or hay, had gathered on the board to form a sheaf. He would then press the rake down firmly, release the stirrup, and slide the corn or hay off the tailboard. The board would be immediately raised again and the process repeated over and over. When there was a heavy crop the shaver's job was by no means an enviable one, especially with the increased speed at which the tractor was moving in comparison to the horse.

At the end of the swathe a lever was pulled forward and the cutting bar would be raised approximately eighteen inches from the ground. The tractor, reaper, and shaver would then make their way around the field to the other side to be ready again for the next swathe. This journey would be made fairly carefully at first until a solid path had been laid. From then on it was our delight to go as fast as the ground would allow, getting the tractor into top gear if possible. My father would be bouncing up and down on the hard iron seat of the reaper like a rubber ball. How he managed to stay on I do not know but he seldom, if ever, complained.

There would always be around ten or twelve men spread out at equal distances along the length of the swathe tying the shaved bundles into sheaves. This was done by using a handful of the longest stalks of the crop itself which were placed around the centre of the bundle and pulled tight, the two ends wrapped together and tucked securely beneath the band.

There would nearly always be time to spare before the reaper arrived back for a new swathe and the ongoing conversation and stories, which had been briefly interrupted, would continue as different pairs met, the last sheaf tucked under their arm. Looking back now it seems to have been more like a day out than the hard day's work that it was.

The best part of the day was around noon when the food arrived. This would normally be signalled by the tinkling sound of the bar being slid open on the gate behind our house, one of the sweetest sounds one could ever imagine! My mother, together with a helper, would be seen coming with a number of large baskets covered with white sheets, and also the large kettle from the kitchen, now being used as a teapot, which was always carried separately. When they arrived in the field all work stopped. The men would each take a sheaf and sit down in a circle. The linen sheets would be spread on the ground in the shade of the hedge, and the food laid out on them, — home made bread and butter, ham, cheese, hard boiled eggs, cakes etc., together with the accompanying cutlery and cups. There is no food ever tasted as nice as the food eaten out in a harvest field. It had a special taste all of its own that could never be replicated anywhere else. Even the tea tasted different. It was a combination, perhaps, of the open air, the scent of the new-mown crop, and the camaraderie of the gathering.

When the food was consumed the pipes would be lit and the next twenty minutes, and sometimes longer, would be filled with conversation and stories. These would deal with events of the day, the amount of harvesting various people had done, the price of cattle, and often feats of the past, especially the amount of corn that some men could cut in a day with a scythe in comparison to the reaper. I still remember vividly a field across the valley from us being pointed out that Joey Hughes R.I.P. had cut with a scythe in a day. This was an almost incredible feat as the field was over an acre and a half, a good day's work even for a reaper. A number present who had witnessed it, however, verified its truth. Others might raise the question if we would be able to get the "cailleh" before nightfall, i.e. if we would manage to finish the harvesting.

The "cailleh" was a corruption of the old Irish word "cailleach", meaning a witch, or a woman from the other world. In this context it always referred to the goddess of the land who permanently watched over the crops. She would keep retreating as the crop was being cut until she was finally trapped in the last piece left standing. This piece was itself called the cailleach.

In the generation previous to ours the cailleach was treated with great reverence. The final stalks of corn, for example, would be cut very carefully and woven into a plait. This would be fixed above the inside of the main door. In the following spring it would be taken down and the grain removed from it and mixed with the seed for the new spring sowing.

Often stories would be told that had a moral edge to them, which caused them to stick in my mind. I remember one occasion on the first day of harvesting when we were cutting corn in Molshey's land, the fields that stretch up towards the mountain from the Crooked Road. Perhaps because it was the first day of the cutting, the help was fairly scarce. One of the people there was Paddy Murphy, or "Bugger Me" as he was always called. He acquired this nickname because he started every story, and very often every sentence, with the words "bugger me". At dinnertime when the sheet was spread in the shelter of Molshey's old house I remarked on the fact that a number of neighbours who had promised to come hadn't turned up and I wondered what had happened to them. Paddy lay back against the old wall and immediately started into a story.

"Well, bugger me", he said, "It reminds me of the lark. One time there was a lark and her young ones who had their nest in a corn field. The young ones were old enough to spend most of their day out playing and often they would wander a good distance from the nest. One evening they came home in a terrible panic and said to their mother, "Hurry, hurry! We must get out of here straight away!" The mother asked them what was the cause of their great panic. The young ones replied that they had heard the farmer talking to the neighbours and making arrangements with them to come the following morning to start to cut the corn.

"Cease your panic," said the mother lark, "We are in no danger. Continue with your play and have no fear."

The following day nothing happened. There was no corn cutting. A few days later the children came home again in an even greater state of agitation. "Quick, quick"! They said. "We must leave now for sure".

"Why is that?" asked the mother lark.

"We heard the farmer talking to the neighbours after mass today," said the children, "and they gave him their solemn promise that they would be here without fail tomorrow morning to start cutting the corn."

"Have no fear", said the mother lark. There is still no danger".

Another four or five days passed uneventfully. The children would come home every evening now quite happy and relaxed. When asked, they would say that there was nothing to report. On the fifth day the mother asked them as usual if they had seen the farmer. They told her that they had but that he wasn't talking to any of the neighbours and that there was no danger. The mother asked them if they had heard him talking to anyone at all. They said that he had just been talking to his son.

"And what did he say?" the mother asked.

"He said that he was fed up waiting on the neighbours and that he was going to start cutting the corn tomorrow himself", said the children.

"Right! Said the mother lark. "Gather all your stuff together. It is time we were getting out of here!"

My father would normally be the first to get up after the meal as he headed off to change the knife in the reaper. He always carried two of these, which he sharpened meticulously every night during the harvest season. It was a very time consuming job as each of the small triangular blades which constituted the knife, twenty per knife, had to be sharpened individually with a three cornered file. It would normally take him over two hours to complete the task. When he was finished the edges would be sparkling and razor sharp.

At the first sound of the reaper the rest would get up and head back to their positions along the swathe. The meal always seemed to have the effect of reviving spirits and the work in the evening, together with the ongoing conversation, would be even more vigorous than in the morning.

When the last swathe was cut and tied all the sheaves throughout the field were "stooked". This was done by standing four sheaves up together, two opposite two, and tying them with a band at the top. This allowed the wind to blow freely through them, drying them out and weathering them.

When the last sheaves were stooked the cutting bar would be raised from the ground for the last time and lifted vertically until it slotted into the iron bar which acted as its stabiliser, keeping it upright. Tractor and reaper would head off through the gap, followed by the working troop. It would not be long until many of them would be meeting again, perhaps even that night, in one of the céilí houses which were dotted throughout the area.

SEEDING

It is strange how things grow
Like seed in the soil
Of the mind to burst
Into grain with surprise
When their autumn arrives.

Small things we ignored,
Like a reaper coaxed out
From the chrysalis of winter,
The line of faces waiting
For the first swathe's miracle,

And the idle chat, dogma of time,
Sheaf cradled on bent arm.
These are the sowings.
Disciples of the mind,
They preached a lesson to be known

Later when their words germinated,
Like old Paddy's story on a bright
Harvest day to the faces reclining
Round the laden sheet spread
Of the wisdom of the lark.

Only now does his lark
Take wings
Soar from that field
To encircle my brain,
Singing Paddy's truth.

The seed is blown down
Through generations in the till
Awaiting the spawn.
Their crop now waves
In my mind, their autumn has come.
I look with wonder at the youth
In my field, playing on my
Headrig, unaware of my seed.

What memory will spring
From the cast of my life? What vision
Take root in their fresh turned sod?
Will my grain sprout here?
Will my lark sing for them?

Reeking and Stacking

In a couple of weeks when the stooks were well dried and weathered the reeking began. A reek was not unlike a small stack, and many would be built throughout the field.

To build a reek you started with a number of stooks which were stacked tightly together until a sufficient width had been reached to form the base of the reek. Then the sheaves were reversed so that the base which had been on the ground was turned outwards. As a result of the way the sheaves had been set in the stook, together with the time spent on the ground, this base was always slightly oblong, with the top end now being slightly shorter than the bottom. As the sheaves were built in their traditional rows clockwise around the top of the prepared base this had the effect of the width of the reek gradually narrowing until it would eventually reach a point, which was secured tightly with a hay, or straw, band.

The height of the reek was always determined by the height of the man building it. It was built from the ground, without use of ladders, rising to the height that the builder could reach. When finished, any loose straws that were lying on the ground were raked up and put over the top of it. It was then roped securely in circles from the tip to just above the base. Our job, as children, was to carry in the stooks for each new reek. Reeking was quite often an urgent job, especially at a time of inclement weather. It was essential to work fast when the stooks were dry to get them built up into the larger units so that the sheaves would be safe from rain. This meant that the reeking would continue long into the evening, being done often by the light of the harvest moon.

Between the middle and the end of September the reeks were drawn by tractor and trailer into the haggard where they were built into large stacks. Each stack was built on a round high "butt" consisting of bushes and whins which had been cut and arranged in the previous week.

The size of the stack was determined by the width of the butt. It was very important that no sheaves were laid on the bare ground as they would be destroyed by dampness. The builder laid the sheaves around in a circle with the short end of the tapering base placed at the bottom. This caused the width of the stack to taper gradually outwards during the first part of its construction. The builder worked on his knees, building two rows at a time. The first was the outer row which had to be placed carefully in line with the upward gradient, the second was placed under his knees approximately eighteen inches back from the outer edge of the first so as to overlap and secure it towards the centre.

There always had to be at least one other person whose job it was to build up the "heart" of the stack. This was a relatively unskilled, though important, job. The sheaves could be placed in any order, provided they kept overlapping the second row in. This was one of the first tasks delegated to us. My father would be reminding us constantly to "keep the heart up!" We already knew the importance of this from the story often told around the hearth of the neighbouring man who was building a stack on his own. He built away and forgot about the heart until he stood up and took a step back and disappeared down through the centre of the stack.

When the stack had reached approximately eight feet high the "ring" would be put on. This was the first row of sheaves where the short side of the base of the sheaves was reversed so as to point upwards. This was the widest part of the stack.

From here the stack kept narrowing, just as in the case of the reek, until it eventually reached a point. When the base of this narrowing point became small enough for the builder to handle the heart on his own the other builder, or builders, left. The last part of the stack was completed by the main builder from the ladder, until it had reached an exact point where the top sheaves were secured tightly with a band.

It required quite a degree of skill to build a stack. The builder was always working "blind" in that he could only see the row he was building and the row below that. He had no way of knowing whether the stack was keeping a perfect gradient. If there was no one else on the ground he would have to go down the ladder and check to ensure that there were no bulges appearing. Up until the ring of the stack all such bulges, together with any sheaves that might be protruding farther than they should, were beaten back into place with the edge of a spade. The importance of this would become clear when the final part of the stack, the thatching, would be completed.

Rushes were used to thatch the stacks. These would have been cut with the scythe in the previous week down in the bog, where they were both plentiful and long. The method of thatching was quite simple. The first circle of thatch was placed above the ring at a position where the ends of the rushes came out well over the ring. The rushes were pushed into the stack by hand, narrow end first. Each succeeding circular row overlapped the row below by six or seven inches. When the top of the stack was reached you had a structure which was not unlike a thatched house, and equally waterproof. The rain would run down the rushes to the ring where it would fall directly to the ground, well out from the base of the stack where it could do no harm, hence the importance of the "spadework" mentioned above.

The completed stack was roped, again in circular fashion, starting from the top. A long pitchfork was used for this purpose, both to guide the rope and also to keep it tight. A haggard full of finished stacks was something to be admired. It had in it a form of native art. Some people were better at building stacks than others and some were acknowledged masters. You would recognise anywhere, for example, a stack built by Pete Kearney. It always had a symmetry and balance that lent it a sense of poised elegance, which was in direct harmony with the landscape in which it was placed.

THE HAGGARD

I remember it now, an autumnal mirage,
Haystacks fattening in the haggard,
The thin glint of rushes
Running up from the hurricane lamp
To an attic of darkness
Where we had hidden the top sheaf,
Tucked tight
In the corner of a September day.
And the God of the harvest
Moving amongst them,
His hurricane lamp panning mysteries
In its shallow light,
Faint glimmers speaking of caverns
That have devoured him
Round endless corners
On his exploration of satisfaction.

We stand waiting for his resurrection
Until his light nudges the darkness
Round some distant stack.
When the path is laid
We too will venture out,
Running hands on stubble
Laid flat against the night,
Headlong into mystery.

The Thrashing

The mill man was one of the most respected men in the area, although respect might not be exactly the right word. It was more fear. He was a man of a fairly short temper who could be quite easily offended. Although he did not own the mill himself he was in sole charge of it and was the final arbiter of all its operations. Since his was the only threshing mill in the area everyone was very careful not to get on his wrong side.

It was not unknown for a farmer to have his gaps opened and his stacks stripped of their ropes and thatch ready for the mill only to find it driving straight past his farm and heading off to someone else because of some grudge, real or imagined, felt by the mill man.

In childhood I thought the mill man to be the most powerful person in the area, almost like a king. I also got the impression, as I watched him operate the engine that pulled the mill, that driving was one of the most difficult jobs a man could undertake. He would be constantly turning the steering wheel, often at a frantic pace, even though he was driving along on the straight. There was a small vertical handle attached to the steering wheel which allowed it to be turned freely and quickly with one hand. This became something of a byword many years later, indeed even today, and was used for criticising someone for an over dramatic use of the steering wheel – "You'd think you were driving the mill!"

It was only later that I realised the reason for this excessive behaviour. Both the large back wheels of the engine and the wide front ones were made of iron. Under any present conventional steering system the wheels would have been almost impossible to turn. The system employed then was quite effective. The serrated end of the steering column sat into a small cup-like mechanism which ensured that the wheels moved only a fraction with each turn of the steering wheel thus leaving the steering relatively easy. However, it required the constant alternate left and right twisting just to keep the machine on the road. In childhood, however, it added considerably to the mystique surrounding the mill man and the whole thrashing experience.

During the thrashing season the mill took precedence over all other activities. No matter how important a task a farmer was engaged in, as soon as the reverberating hum of the mill reached him along the valley he would drop the task immediately, sling his pitchfork over his shoulder, and head off in the direction of the sound of the mill. The reason was very simple. The thrashing was a job that no family could do on their own. It took quite a number of men to perform all the essential tasks and each farmer was relying on his neighbours to gather to help him when his turn came. It was essential, therefore, that he "earned the swap".

When our thrashing day arrived there would be a great deal of excitement. My mother would have been getting food in for a couple of days previously and anything that could be prepared in advance would be ready. My father would have all the gaps open and the pathway into the haggard cleared and levelled. Early on the morning of the thrashing he would strip the stacks of their ropes and thatch.

When the iron clad engine pulling the long and, to us towering, mill finally arrived it was an impressive sight. It took a great deal of skill to guide the whole mass from the road in through the fairly narrow entrance to the yard. The steering wheel would be in full flight but the mill man always looked calmly in control. He rarely ever spoke and the questions of those fussing about trying to help were ignored. He was a man who knew his business.

When the mill was guided up the yard and the front was turned in towards the haggard two large stones were placed behind the back wheels. The engine would be disengaged and reversed to the rear of the mill where it would be attached by a thick straight pushing bar. From here on the steering had to be done by two or three men who would take up the triangular tow bar at the front and, using all the force that they could muster, guide the front wheels as the mill was inched forward from the rear until it would be in exactly the right position in the haggard to "catch", if possible, all the stacks that had to be thrashed.

Next the built-in spirit level on the side of the mill had to be checked to make sure it was exactly level. If not, adjustments were made; either shallow holes dug, or flat stones placed, and the mill inched backwards until a precise level was achieved. Large stones were then placed behind and in front of the rear wheels preventing any movement. The pushing bar was then removed and the thick wide driving belt which was always carried rolled up on the back of the engine was taken down and unfurled.

One end of the belt was placed around the flywheel on the left side of the mill. It was then given a half turn and the other end was placed around the drive wheel on the engine. The engine was then moved back gradually until the required tension was achieved on the belt. The reason for the half turn was to ensure that the belt did not slip off the drive wheel. As the inside of the belt was always touching it would have a sheen as though it had just been honed and polished.

The fold-away extension flaps along both sides of the top of the mill were folded outwards and the iron supports beneath them slotted into the keepers provided for the purpose on the sides of the mill. This provided a wide platform onto which the sheaves could be pitched. It was here that the "losers" stood, those who opened the sheaves and passed them to the "feeder". The latter's job was to insert them seed-end first into the opening leading to the spinning mill-drum. Behind this opening there was a recessed standing place, approximately waist deep, in which the feeder stood. This was to ensure that he could not fall, or be pulled, into the mill. His was the most dangerous job at the thrashing.

When all was ready the mill was started, sending out its summoning call. In about ten minutes enough neighbours would have gathered to start the thrashing. Normally the hay would be thrashed first as there would be much less of it than the corn, usually only one fairly small stack.

During the trashing the seed was channelled to the end of the mill, through four slots positioned approximately three feet from the ground. Each of these slots had a vertical sliding hatch door which allowed them to be opened and closed easily. At the rear of each slot were two metal hooks, and one at the front. The tops of the bags for catching the seed would be placed through the rear hooks. The front of the bags would then be pulled tight around the slots, overlapped, and run through the front hook. As each bag was filled its slot would be closed and another one opened. This allowed time for the full bags to be removed and placed to one side and new empty bags attached.

The men in charge of the bags had an easy time when the hay was being thrashed. Hayseed was very small and light and it took quite a while for a bag to fill and, when filled, the bags were easy to handle. It was a different story when the trashing of the corn started, especially if it was a high yield crop. Two slots would then be in constant use. The bags were a great deal heavier and quite awkward to unhook and lift to one side. It was often a race to get this done and get new bags on before the other two had filled. This was more so the case if you found yourself on your own in charge of the bags, as happened to me a number of years later. As I struggled to get the full bags away I could see the other bags getting fuller and fuller. You couldn't close the slots as the grain would back up and clog the whole process, and it was unthinkable to just let it pour out on to the ground. It was a panic-filled experience!

There would be two or three men in charge of carrying the seed up the concrete steps to the loft. The hayseed would be left in the bags unemptied, to be later sieved and sold. The corn, however, would be emptied out on the loft floor, which would have been cleared and thoroughly swept a couple of days previously, and the empty bags returned to the mill. There would always be two men pitching from the stacks onto the mill where the losers opened the sheaves and threw them over to the feeder. If the last stack was out of reach of the mill the sheaves were pitched from it onto the middle stack and from there onto the mill. Although laborious, this was much preferable to the major task that would be involved in moving the mill again.

Often enough there would be a pileup of sheaves on the mill platform and the feeder would be shouting to "take it easy"! If the sheaves were not fed in seed-first the whole exercise would be pointless as they would not have the seed removed. The thrashed hay and straw was churned out by a mechanism that resembled kicking feet at the extreme end of the top of the mill. It was the job of the forkers to keep this area cleared. The thrashed material was carried by them to be built on new butts which had been prepared a couple of days previously on the right hand side of the haggard.

The hay was built in a single stack, being pitched up to the builder who used both his arms to build and his pitchfork to shape the growing stack.

The straw was always built in a long, wide rick. There were always at least two men building this. As in the case of the seed, the straw was much bulkier than the hay, and the forkers were kept very busy keeping the mill area cleared. When the rick reached a height where the forkers could no longer pitch the straw to the builders, ladders were placed against the side of the rick. Men stood on these facing outwards. Each forkful of straw was reached up to them and they in turn forked it over their heads onto the rick. They were always working "blind" and would be covered with straw and dust, in their eyes and down their backs. Next to the feeder, this was the hardest job at the mill.

When the thrashing was in full swing the haggard would be in constant motion, with people moving in all directions, some covered in the unending cloud of chaff being blown out from the mill. If an untrained observer were watching he might well think that it was a scene of complete chaos. However, it was a chaos that was at all times under control. Each man there knew exactly what his role was and he fulfilled it with an expertise that to him was mere routine.

Inside in the house as dinner time approached the two halves of the polished American table, which always stood in two separate rooms, were brought into the kitchen and joined together. These had been brought home from America by my father's uncle many years before and were treasured items. As a single unit they filled almost all the available space. The kitchen was what nowadays, I suppose, would be called the dining room. No such names existed at that time. Each household had a kitchen where everyone sat at night and where meals were eaten on special occasions, and a back-kitchen where the meals were cooked, and eaten on normal days. The large table seated fourteen and there would always be at least two full sittings.

This was the only time that the mill man would relax and loosen up a little. The women would be fussing around him and carrying on what could only be called a mild flirtation. They would ask him how he was getting on with "the widow". When the mill man would protest, with a smile breaking on his face, that he didn't know what they were talking about they would nudge him and keep at him — "Aw, you're the sly one! You think we don't know what you're up to, you and the widow. We have our spies, you know!

By this time the mill man would be chuckling with delight as he played his role in this double game that was played out every year. I don't know why it was always "the widow" that he was supposed to be having the affair with. However it always put the mill man in good form and set him up for the rest of the evening.

In the afternoon the highlight of the day came as the stacks came closer and closer to the butts. Like the "Cailleach", all the rats and mice that had taken up residence in the stacks kept moving inwards towards the centre as their surroundings diminished. As the pitcher stuck his fork into the last sheaves of each stack everyone who was on the ground, including any dogs that were on the farm, would be gathered around. As the last sheaves were whipped away there would be an eruption of rats and mice cascading in all directions to the shouts of men and children and the barking of dogs in hot pursuit. Although many met their waterloo in the combined onslaught a healthy number always escaped, enough at least to ensure the future welfare of the species!

When the thrashing was complete and the mill had been swept down, re-shuttered, and reversed safely out of the haggard and back onto the road to continue on its rounds, there were still a couple of jobs to do. The first, which was always done by us children, was the gathering together of the large mound of chaff. We stuffed this into the empty bags and stored it on the loft to be used later as bedding, especially in the henhouses. The other job, which was done by my father and a couple of close neighbours who stayed behind, was the raking down, covering, and roping of the stacks. All the loose rushes that had formed the thatch of the previous stacks were used for the covering, thrown up and guided into place with the pitchforks.

The large rick of straw was always roped crossways, each rope being rolled into a ball, one end held as the ball was thrown high over the top and down the other side. Each end was weighed down with a stone, thus ensuring a constant downward tension as the straw settled down over time. These would be put approximately eighteen inches apart the full length of the rick.

There was always a sense of satisfaction and relief when the thrashing was over; relief because it was the most complex task of the harvest season and subject to many hazards, not least of which was the unpredictability of the weather; and satisfaction as it marked the end of the farming year and guaranteed security for the future, for at least another year. However, unknown to anyone then, great changes were lurking in the background, changes that were destined to cause a major disruption in this seemingly timeless and stable way of life. With the ongoing and inexorable demise of the small farmers, who were not being replaced, and the eventual arrival of, first the binder, and later the combined harvester the rural scene was utterly transformed. No longer would groups of men be seen working in field or haggard. The reaping, stacking, thrashing, were all now obsolete. The mill man was stripped of his crown and shrank to his normal size, a small, thin, and suddenly insignificant man. Deprived now of all his power and mystique he lived out the rest of his days in a meagre existence, almost unnoticed.

Today things have progressed even further. No longer will you see fields of ripening corn waving in the wind or potato blossoms opening in the sun. Very seldom will you even see a ploughed field and, if you do, it is always merely for the purpose of reseeding the ground for new grass. The small farms have virtually all disappeared, either sold off into larger units, or let out in conacre, the next generation who should have been running them now off with university degrees in the large cities running the world. All that remains is the memory, enshrined in hills and mountain fields.

RHYTHMNS

Words lie on these mountains,
Stone syllables before me,
Honed into rhythm
Beneath my people's hands.

They walked these hills composing
Their text in mountain ditches,
Their syntax tracing ridges
Governing from the past.

I now walk these mountains,
Their stones whispering verses,
Assonance of pathways
That rhythms me to them.

The Céilí House

Let me say first of all that the term "céilí house" had nothing to do with dancing. The term comes from the more basic meaning of the word céilí, i.e. a social gathering. And that is exactly what it was.

During the long winter months, at a time when there was no electricity, television, or even radio, the men used go three or four nights per week "on their céilí" to various neighbouring houses and while away the hours chatting and conversing. As far back as I can remember our house was a céilí house. At that time there was no such thing as locked doors, or invitations required, or even the necessity to knock. I can't recall a time when there was ever a lock, or even a bar, on our own front door.

The men just walked straight in and took their place with the rest around the open fire. The céilí house was an integral part of the way of life in the rural society of South Armagh, almost its backbone, stretching back long before living memory, just as it was in the Gaelic speaking areas of Donegal. It acted almost like a local news media where reports of all the important events occurring in the area, particularly an illness or a death, spread swiftly throughout the whole neighbourhood.

In addition to this the topics discussed in the céilí house were wide-ranging, covering all the pressing matters of the day, especially the current state of the harvesting, the forthcoming weather, the rising or falling prices of pigs, horses, calves, and, at Christmas time, turkeys. The latter was of crucial interest to the women, as virtually every housewife would have a brood of turkeys raised and fattened for the Christmas market. On this she depended heavily for the provision of the Christmas fare for the family.

The repertoire of the céilí house also, of course, included stories, the thing in which we delighted most as children, especially stories about events that had been witnessed first hand by the teller and had a clear ring of authenticity about them. Such stories included, for example, the blow by blow account of how Mick McGinnis, by then an elderly man who lived a short distance up the road from us, had single handilly beaten three men who had attacked him in a pub in Liverpool when he was in his prime, and he with only the use of one arm, the other one having been broken in a previous fight; or the story of Pete Kearney's father carrying five hundred weight of seed corn, a two hundred weight bag on each shoulder and a hundred under his arm, from the top of Sturgan brae to Campbell's bridge, a distance of approximately a quarter of a mile. He did this so as not to disturb the work going on preparing a field at the bridge for sowing by having to loose the horse out of the harrow; or the tale of the widow Flanagan burning stones on Hannigan's hill, an ancient druidic ritual, to curse the local money lender; or the story told by Pat O'Brien, who could never be beaten for the extravagance of his tales, of how, while working as a navvy in London during the war, he took down a German fighter plane with his shovel!

In addition to these there would be many stories told about matchmaking. Such a one concerned a local, fairly naïve man, called Michael Atkinson, and the time that he was keenly in the market for a woman. Some of the "wise boys" took him up to Kate Boyle's house where there were twelve daughters. They told him, since the choice was so wide, that he should be able to get at least one of them. When they arrived outside the house they told Michael, who was clutching the obligatory bottle of whiskey, to wait outside the door until they went inside to "square things up" with Kate and let her know that he was coming. They went around the side of the house, jumped over the ditch, nipped across the upper field and back out on the road again above where Michael was positioned. They turned their coats inside out and, pulling their caps down well over their eyes, they came sauntering down the road. They asked Michael in a gruff accent what he was doing and when he told them they launched into him with a volley of verbal abuse asking him who did he think he was coming up to their country to steal the women off them! They took the bottle of whiskey from him, gave him a couple of good scuffs around the lugs and sent him on his way back home. They then went into Kate Boyle's where they had a great nights céilíng on the bottle of whiskey.

It is interesting to note that this man managed to find a wife a number of years later. A more reliable matchmaker brought him to a house where there were two daughters. The elder of the two was very plain and quite staid, but the younger one was the complete opposite. She was beautiful and vivacious. Michael, of course, tried for "the young one" and he couldn't believe his luck when he managed to make the match. The date was fixed for the wedding and Michael went home on cloud nine. During the next couple of weeks he could scarcely contain himself, counting the very hours to the big event. When the day finally arrived and the bride walked up the isle to join Michael at the altar rails he chanced a sidelong glance at her and his heart missed a beat. He leaned over to the best man, who happened to be the bride's brother and over six foot tall, and whispered to him —"This is not the one I picked!" The best man bent down and hissed in his ear, "Shut your mouth or I'll break your gob!" The wedding went ahead and, as it happened, Michael spent just over twenty-five years of very happy married life with the "plain one", until she unfortunately died. On the occasions when stories were told they wouldn't normally start until later on in the night after all other business had been covered, by which time we would have already been packed off to bed in the upper room which led off from the kitchen. However, the seating arrangements in the kitchen were such that a large armchair with a high back was positioned across at an angle to the open door of the bedroom. This meant that we could slip out of bed and crawl along the floor unnoticed and curl up behind the chair. Here we spent many long hours captivated by the stories.

There was an art in telling a story well and always a certain amount of thinly veiled rivalry between those contending for the reputation of best storyteller. One of the most effective tools the storyteller had in his armoury was the pipe.

At that time nearly everyone smoked the pipe, which took a considerable amount of time to fill and light, something which proved very useful at certain times. A lot of the stories were heard before but people always delighted in hearing them again and they nearly always got better with each telling.

Storytelling was a two-way event in which the audience was expected to play its part. At critical points in the story when the storyteller would pause, the audience was expected to ask the appropriate question to further the action — " And what did you do, Peter, to get out of such an awful fix?" — or "And who was responsible, Peter? Did they ever catch him?"

And Peter would reply, "Well, I'll tell you that just right now!" He would then proceed to stretch out towards the open fire with a piece of paper in his hand and start to light his pipe, leaving everyone suspended on the edge of expectation. It was only when the pipe would be fully operational, which required a considerable amount of effort and time that he would continue.

There was one man in the area who had the distinction of going on his céilí twice a day, first in the morning and again later on in the evening. His name was Mickey Murphy, or the Coinne as he was always called. Most of the people in the district had a nickname, especially the Murphys and the Mc Parlands because they were so numerous. It was a practical way of distinguishing between them. Nearly all the nicknames had their origin in Irish, Mickey's coming from the Irish word "coinín" meaning "a rabbit", most likely from his agility, especially in hopping over ditches. His house stood on an elevated site across the valley from us and we had a clear view of him as he headed off on his first tour.

The Coinne was one of the most delightful people who ever came into our house. He was never ever in bad form and always had a smile on his face. He had an airy, carefree manner which was immediately infectious. Any troubles you might have had were forgotten as soon as he came in through the door.

During the morning round we would be sitting, or eating, in the back kitchen which had an open fire and a pair of bellows, one of the most effective heating systems ever devised. The Coinne would get seated in the corner and start blowing the bellows until the fire would be roaring up the chimney. This first visit was more of a curtsey call and never involved any in-depth discussion. That would come later in the evening together with the stories. At this stage he dealt with lighter subjects. He would often speak jokingly of the various women he could get if he went to the trouble of asking them, bursting into spasms of song as he went. There was one particular woman whom he really did seem to have a notion of and her name would be mentioned often, with my mother constantly urging him to go and ask her. His reply would always be the same, that he would be doing the asking "any of these days".

During the latter part of his life he would talk wistfully, with a sparkle in his eye, of all the women he could have got if he had really wanted them. The Coinne's life seemed to be an idyllic one. He very seldom had any work to do. In the spring he would buy cattle and fatten them on his hill farm during the Summer. As he had only himself to keep this was quite sufficient. Not for him ploughing or cropping or thrashing. We often used to say to him that he was the only "gentleman farmer" in Lislea, something with which he would readily agree with a hearty laugh.

Someone once told Mickey that the view alone from his house was worth a thousand pounds. That was at a time when a thousand pounds was more like a million today. This gave him a great deal of pride and often when he would be leaving from his morning round he would stand at our door looking across at his house, rolling the words around in his mouth as he spoke, almost tasting them, "The view alone is worth a thousand pounds!" and with that he would be off down the road lilting a song, a man without a trouble in the world.

MICKEY

You'd see him coming down
The fields,
Feet kissing stone ditches
Hand pressing their spine
As he headed for
McCann's
Or Pat O'Brien's
On his daily rounds.
No man ever cultivated the art
Of wasting time
With such devotion.
Bulldozing gloom
With iron wit

Sharp to the touch
The house rang with his presence.

When our turn came
Late in the evening
We'd slip from the room
Breath bated
Behind the chair
Embezzling moments
Of sheer joy
From the day's takings
To be spent later
As our father squared his position
On the torn couch
To receive the deluge
Of his recent humour

Later
When the ditches revolted
And gaps were broken
In their bony ridges
To let him through
I knew Mickey
With the felon truth
Of adult knowledge,
His hooped body
Wrung by the twist
Of his many sorrows;
Spoke his courage.

And I played his game
In earnest
Fellow conspirator
In his life's lie
As I drank his face
And hooked nose

And eyes sparkling
To a background
Of barren hills
And an empty house
Whitewashed against gloom.

And I know his truth now
More real
From a distance
Of many miles
Unbroken
By the courage of his smile.

The time of year would always arrive in the céilí house, especially around Halloween, for the inevitable ghost stories. These were the stories which both delighted and terrified us the most. We would huddle behind the armchair as the open fire sent large shadows dancing around the walls, the fear and excitement running in tingles down our backs. The great thing about these stories for us was that the vast majority of them were told first-hand, by the very people who had actually experienced the events. This brought them out of the realm of fantasy and into the reality of fact.

Stories, such as, on his way home from his céilí late at night, Michael Murphy met a stranger on the Ballard Road. Having stopped and spoken to him briefly he moved on. After a couple of paces when he turned around there was no one there. The man had completely disappeared; or the time when the uncle of one of the men went to bed as usual up in the bedroom only to find when he woke up in the morning that both himself and the bed were down in the kitchen. This happened three nights in a row. On the fourth day the uncle left the house and never slept in it again; or the time when the priest's horse refused to cross a small bridge on the Longfield road as he was returning from a sick call. Despite all the priest's efforts the horse refused to move until he finally got down off its back, knelt down on the road and prayed and at last coaxed him forward. When he arrived home the horse was covered in a white lather of foam. The next morning he was found lying dead in the stable; and also the time that three men on their way home from their céilí in our house around half twelve at night stood transfixed as a beautiful child danced before them in the moonlight along the wall of Lislea graveyard. When they finally summoned up enough courage to move forward, the child disappeared.

It is hard to over estimate the importance of the céilí house in the Ring of Gullion area in those early years, right up indeed to the 1960's, and the significant role it played in rural society. These were people whose life was by no means easy, a life of almost constant daily toil. The céilí house was the only means of relief and entertainment that they had. Without it their lives would have been a great deal poorer.

Like the many jobs done on the farm, such as the corn cutting and the thrashing, the céilí house also provided a form of communal bonding, where men could meet others of their kind with the same range of interests. It was almost like a local parliament where critical issues of the day were debated in detail, opinions put forward and tested, and values reinforced. The art of conversation and storytelling were honed to a fine edge, helped greatly by a language that owed much more to its recent Gaelic past than it did to the so-called "English" that we thought we were speaking, carrying with it as it did the rhythm, colour, and poetic nuances of the original. These were men who lived life at a completely different pace than today, a pace dictated by the horse and the single score plough. For them there was plenty of time to embellish their language and sharpen up their stories along the headrigs of the day for the cut and thrust of the céilí house at night where reputations could be won or lost. Unknown to themselves, they were not only skilled artisans, but also scholars, dramatists, philosophers, poets. In a later era I have no doubt that some of them at least would have been numbered amongst the academics of their day.

I could never have imagined as I watched these men "spoked" around the fire each night in the céilí house "planting their tales in each other's till" that I was witnessing the end of an era, unfolding literally before my eyes. I am not saying, by any means, that life today is any worse, or indeed better, but it definitely is different! I count myself fortunate to have been able to spend the early years of my youth, before I could be waylaid by education, in the company of these people. They were destined later to represent for me the true university of life and wisdom. They passed from this world, one by one, almost unnoticed and unsung.

BETRAYAL

Lislea graveyard
Is the published book
Of my verse,
Each printed death
An unuttered poem
Of my life.

I read them as I pass
Dumb-tongued
To the Crooked Road
Punctuating their text,
Each rock and corner
A pause
Where my words were struck,
Phrases formed
By a raised stick
Or a flung head,
Silent poets of
A timeless verse.

I have betrayed them
To the chiselled stone,
Vocal chords of death,
Unsung,
They publish my neglect.

Organic Farming — Farming as it was.

Throughout the years of my childhood and youth, from the 1940's to the 1960's, all the farmers in South Armagh were engaged in organic farming, although they didn't know it. They were merely following the traditional farming patterns that had been established long before and had been followed consistently for countless generations. These patterns were eco-friendly and allowed the land to breathe at its own natural pace. Intensive farming was still far off in the future. At this time artificial fertilisers were virtually unknown. The one form in which they existed was the bagged potash, which was necessary in small amounts for the potatoes. The people always referred to this as "potato manure", or, more frequently, "bag-stuff".

Virtually all the foodstuff fed to the animals was home-produced. The sheep were left out on grass for most of the winter until they came close to lambing and were fed hay, together with crushed corn and barley.

Throughout the winter months the cattle were housed. They were fed hay and straw as fodder. In addition, we always set approximately an acre of either kale or turnips. These were left in the ground and used as required. The kale was around two and a half feet tall with a thick stem and wide leaves, which remained green throughout the winter. It was a very arduous task on a cold winter's day, with frost or snow on the ground, to have to go out and cut the kale. A rope would be spread on the ground and the cut kale piled on top of it until there would be as much as you could carry. The rope would then be tightened and the bundle slung on your back and carried up to the yard.

This part of the job was hard enough, but a much more difficult task was getting the kale up to the cows' heads. As soon as you entered the byre they could smell it and would start twisting and turning in all directions, sometimes breaking their tying chains, to get at it. The kale was just thrown uncut in the shallow feeding trough at their heads. You could almost hear the sap running in the kale as they munched their way through it.

In the case of turnips, the job was more difficult. They had to be pulled from the ground and "snedded". This involved cutting off firstly the root and all outgrowths so that all traces of clay were removed from the bottom of the turnip and then cutting off the top stalk. On a cold day the power would be almost gone from your hands by the time the snedding was finished. The turnips were then put into meal bags and carried up to the yard. Here they were put into a pulper, a simple machine operated by turning a handle which drove a serrated cylinder which cut the turnips up into small pieces. Buckets were placed in turn beneath the bottom outlet to collect the pulped material. This was fed to the cows, at approximately half a bucketful per cow. Their reaction to it was the same as to the kale.

Throughout the winter months the large outside boiler would be in constant use. This was a wide iron boiler built into a block surround. It held two hundredweight of potatoes and was normally boiled twice per week. The clay would be washed off the potatoes, normally in a large bath, using a wooden beetle to swish them around in the water, and then filled into the boiler, a bath-full at a time. When full, clean water would be added and the boiler would be covered with a heavy, tight-fitting iron lid.

In the block surround there was a space, running the full length of the underside of the boiler, for a fire. This would be lit and fed with both logs and coal until the potatoes were boiled. This normally took about two hours. The fire was then raked out and any remaining water was drained from the boiler. The lid was then removed to allow the potatoes to "teem", i.e. for all the steam and moisture to dry off. They were then mashed with the wooden beetle into something approaching champ.

This was fed to the cattle, nearly always in the morning, mixed with crushed corn. It was also fed to the pigs, mixed, normally, with skimmed milk. Occasionally, when the farm produce was used up, mostly in the summertime, dairy meal, and sometimes pig meal, would be bought in.

Churning

Like a large number of other farmers, we sent milk to the creamery. The cows were milked night and morning. The buckets of milk were taken in and placed in the cooler in the milk-house. This was a simple block-built trough, which was filled with cold water every day.

When the milk was cooled it was poured through a sieve into the large milk can. Every morning this was carried to the roadside in the front of the house, where it was picked up by the milk lorry, and the can, or cans, from the previous day were left off. Everyone had a registered number with the creamery. This was printed on all the cans so that there could be no confusion.

Enough milk would always be kept back to supply all the household needs. In addition, each day some cream would be taken from the top of the milk and put into an earthenware crock which always stood beside the wall in the milk house. When the crock was full, normally once per week, the cream would be churned.

The churns were tall, wooden, barrel-like structures, narrowing towards the middle and widening out again at the top. There was a wooden lid with a hole in the middle, which came down over the long handle of the staff which was used to do the churning. There was a certain amount of mystique, and indeed superstition, surrounding churning. It would happen very occasionally that for some reason, which no one could ever work out, the butter would not form. The old people believed that this was caused by someone, normally a jealous or spiteful neighbour, putting the evil eye on the churning to take away the butter. There was, indeed, a certain reverence associated with all things involving milk. People were always very careful not to spill it, or waste it in any way. Also, if anyone ever came into a byre where milking was in progress they would always say, "God bless the work!" The same applied in a house where churning was taking place. Here, also, the newcomer would normally be expected to take a turn at the churning, to have a "brash" as they called it. Most did it readily. Some would be a little reticent, in case the butter didn't form and they would in some way be held responsible. The old superstition of "the evil eye" was still strong.

Churning was by no means an easy job. It would be very difficult for one person to continue plunging and raising the staff throughout the whole process, which lasted for around three quarters of an hour, without a number of breaks. As children we were always called into service to do our turn. It was very important that the same rhythm was maintained to keep the milk at a constant temperature. At different times the lid would be raised a little and water would be poured around the inside walls of the churn.

After churning away with the staff for a long period of time with no apparent change taking place, and no sign that there ever would be, it always came as a surprise to feel the milk suddenly starting to thicken beneath the staff. After another couple of minutes an increased weight could be sensed on the staff. The lid would then be raised and there on the top of the milk would be a thick layer of butter. It is easy to understand why the old people had attached so much mysticism to this process. It did seem as if the butter materialised almost by magic. Indeed, if no butter formed at all it would have seemed somehow more natural. Like in so many other cases, one is left to wonder how people ever discovered this process.

All the butter would now be collected together carefully with the base of the staff and put into a large dish. This would be filled with clean, cold water on as many occasions as necessary until all the milk was washed out of the butter. The latter was now pressed out flat in the dish and a fairly liberal helping of salt was sprinkled over it. The butter was then mixed by hand until the salt was spread evenly through it. It was now time to divide the butter up into "prints".

This was done with the use of a fairly broad, flat platter and a round mould with a handle underneath it. The mould would have a pattern of some type, mostly flowers. A portion of butter would be lifted from the dish with the platter and placed on the top of the mould. The butter would then be shaped around the mould with the platter and tapped flat on the top. The mould of butter would then be turned out on a plate, with the moulded design clearly showing on the top. This was called a "print of butter". There would be quite a number of prints from a full churning, enough to last about a week and a half.

Bread would be baked most days on the griddle over the open fire. The buttermilk, the residue of the churning, would be used for this purpose. A piece of fresh baked griddle bread covered with a liberal helping of new homemade butter was something the likes of which is not to be found anywhere today. There is nothing that even comes close to it!

I never recall shop butter, or creamery butter as it was called, ever coming into our house up until the late 1960's. The same applied to bread. My grandmother R.I.P., who lived in Ballard, would come for her pension to Lislea Post Office every Monday. Most weeks she would come the short distance up the hill to visit us and she always brought with her a farmhouse loaf, the old pre-sliced kind with the hard crust. This was a great novelty to us as children. We always called it "the pension loaf".

Fresh buttermilk was delicious to drink. It had a sharp tangy taste that not only slaked your thirst but also revived your senses. Our parents would always be warning us to be careful and not to drink too much of it, or drink it too fast, as it could "curdle" in our stomachs. As well as drinking it, my father would pour some of it into a dish and wash his face with it. When I first saw him doing this I could scarcely believe it. My father, a hardworking farmer was not one who was ever known for taking any particular care of himself, nor would he have time for anyone who did. When I asked him about this he said that it was the old tradition, practised by his own people. When my father died at the age of seventy-six his skin was as fresh and clear as it was when I first knew him.

Roaming Hens

My mother always kept around two hundred hens. There was a small field below the house given over to them, where three quite large henhouses stood. Throughout the day they had the free run of the field, and, indeed, many of the adjoining fields as well, as it wasn't possible at that time to erect fences high enough to keep them in. At feeding time, as soon as my mother called them, they came flying from all directions.

They were fed corn, which my mother scattered broadcast on the grass. As she walked the hens packed in tight around her, so that she looked as if she were moving through a white sea.

There were laying boxes in all the houses. In many of these there would be a delph egg placed to encourage the hens to lay there. The vast majority did, but there would always be a few rogue individuals who preferred to follow nature's way and make their nests out in the open. One of our ongoing tasks as children was to go looking for such nests throughout the summer months, the nests of hens that were "laying out".

This was a time consuming task but also one that had a certain sense of excitement about it. You would never know exactly where you might find such a nest. Along the ditches there would be a lot of undergrowth and also nettles, which provided cover. You would have to go along with a stick pulling back the undergrowth carefully and looking in the hedge. The majority of the time your efforts would be in vain but then, out of the blue, you would turn back an innocent looking piece of undergrowth and there before you would be a neatly made nest full of eggs, tucked tight in under the hedge. It was as if you had gained access to a hidden world. On one occasion I discovered a nest in the haggard, which was the most frequent haunt of the hens laying out, which contained just over two dozen eggs. That rogue had managed to go for most of the season without ever being detected. A common threat to the hens in this type of lifestyle was the fox. Our land was almost adjacent to the mountain where foxes could be clearly heard calling to each other at night. They sounded almost like dogs barking. During the daytime we always had to keep a constant look out for them.

However, this wasn't always successful. I still remember clearly one occasion when a fox entered the field right behind our house in broad daylight and grabbed a hen. He caught her by the neck and threw her over his shoulder. My father ran after him as fast as he could and a neighbouring man ran at an angle to his path with a spade to try and cut him off. The hen was quite large and a heavy weight for the fox. As I watched from the top of the Chapel brae, where I had a panoramic view, I expected him to drop the hen any moment as my father was gradually catching up. But he didn't. He cleared the ditch, beating both men, made it across the adjoining field and disappeared into the mountain, the hen still slung neatly across his shoulder. There was something fascinating, almost haunting, about the scene, which has remained with me to this day. I still admire his style!

When darkness began to fall all the hens would start to gather from their respective directions and take up their places in the different houses where they would roost for the night. The doors would be securely locked. The eggs were always lifted from the laying boxes in the early evening. A lorry came to collect them once per week. Before that they had to be cleaned, a job that was always done by my mother. They could not be put in water but had to be cleaned "dry". This was done with a cloth and white scouring powder. It was an extremely slow and tedious job. When cleaned, the eggs were placed in vertical layers in cardboard holders in a large box. This box held thirty dozen in all. My mother would always have at least a box and a half for collection each week.

The hens themselves were all home produced. My mother had a large incubator in which she hatched the eggs. This was kept indoors in the bottom room, as it required constant attention. The hatching eggs were bought from a section of the Department of Agriculture, which most likely doesn't exist now. The incubator was heated with four oil lamps contained in special compartments around the sides. They were positioned in such a way that the heat spread evenly through the incubator. It was critical that the temperature was kept at a certain level and that the eggs were turned frequently. It was fascinating as a child watching through the glass surround as the eggs hatched. The first thing that you would see was a small chip appearing in the eggshell, and the tip of a tiny beak. This would be followed by other chips, normally around in a circle, large enough to allow the chick to break through. The first thing that would appear was its head and neck. It would normally take a rest at this stage, and survey its surroundings with an almost quizzical expression, the round section of eggshell often still perched on the top of its head like a small hat. It would finally, with much struggling, complete its emergence and lie panting on top of the un-hatched eggs. At this stage it was wet and ungainly looking, barely resembling a chick at all.

On the end wall of the incubator, directly opposite the incubating tray, there was a small window, which allowed the light from one of the heating lamps to shine through. As soon as each chick had dried out sufficiently to find its feet it headed directly towards this light. However, the hatching tray was a few inches short of the full length of the incubator, so that when the chick came to the edge it automatically tumbled down a short distance into a much larger holding tray that ran the full length of the incubator. As the eggs hatched this gradually filled up with chirping chicks, quickly drying out into fluffy balls of golden wonder.

This was almost like a self-regulating conveyor belt of production. You never knew when you went to bed at night what changes the morning would bring; what number of the inert eggs lying at the top would have been transformed into the miracle of chirping life below. When all the eggs were hatched, which was normally completed inside a couple of days, the next task was to divide the chicks into males and females. This was something which it was almost impossible for an untrained person to do. At that age there were no obvious distinguishing features, physical or otherwise, to separate them.

The "sexing" of the chicks was done by a lady from the Ministry of Agriculture who was specially trained for the job. Once summoned, she would come to the house, carrying with her nothing but her expertise. She was tall and dark, with a strong firm jaw and had a great sense of presence and authority. She spoke with a sharp nasal inflection, which added to her mystique. She would sit down with a flourish and launch into her task with a brusque certainty.

As she spoke briskly about all the topics of the day the chicks would be flying through her hands, each given barely a glance, and tossed unceremoniously into two cardboard boxes, females to the left, males to the right. She had the type of authority that was not to be questioned, like a solicitor or a Parish Priest. At sexing chickens it was clear that she was the master. The whole point of the incubating exercise was to end up with as many females as possible. With each chick that landed in the right-hand box my mother would let out a silent groan. You felt, however, that if the whole brood were to end up in this box the sexing lady would still have swept out of the house as usual, coat flying and unquestioned.

The male chicks were kept separate from the females and fed a different diet. Their future was to be fattened, either for sale to the "hen-man" from Newry, or for the home table. The females were put in a small house outside with a wired-off run. They were fed on special meal pellets and greens, such as dandelions, which were pulled and tied in bunches from the wire mesh. When large enough they were transferred into the "pullet-houses", where they had a free run of the fields. When they were ready to start laying they were put into the hen houses to replace the older hens, which were sold off to the hen-man. And so the cycle was maintained, apart from the odd unforeseen disruption.

Such a one occurred when I was about fifteen years of age. My mother came into the house one morning in great distress, which was a fairly unusual occurrence. She said that a fox had got at the pullets. I went out to investigate, expecting to find one or two of them dead. That year my mother had a large number of chickens, which were now fully reared and ready to be transferred to the henhouses.

When I entered the first house I couldn't believe my eyes. Virtually all the pullets were dead, lying scattered on the floor and on the roosting perches, each with its neck broken. The few that survived looked completely disorientated. The fox had burrowed his way down through the clay from the outside and up through the earthen floor on the inside. When I went to each of the other two houses the same scene awaited me. Of the whole brood, less than a quarter were alive. I spent the whole day drawing them in barrow-loads to be buried. I had always heard that a fox would only kill what he needs. This event would seem to contradict that long-held theory. It was a total massacre.

The Dunghill

The critical factor in the success of all farming at that time was the home produced fertiliser, in the form of the manure stored in the dunghill. During the long winter months when the cattle were all inside, the byres were cleaned out daily. There was a floor recess approximately two feet wide by nine inches deep running the full length of each byre, just behind the cattle, which were always tied. This was called the group. This trapped and retained all the manure. Every morning, seven days per week, this was cleaned out with shovel, brush, and wheelbarrow and transported to the dunghill which was always fairly close to the outhouses. All the manure from the pig houses was also added.

As the winter progressed the dunghill would grow in size quite quickly. It was always necessary to keep squaring the sides so that the growing pile remained fairly restricted. A shallow indentation was normally left at the top to catch and hold moisture, which was necessary for fermentation. By the springtime when the cattle were let out to grass the dunghill would have grown to a dramatic size, taking up most of the space in the yard leading to the haggard. It was so large that you could scarcely imagine it ever being cleared.

When the potato field was ready, with the drills opened, each farmer started to shift his dunghill. In our case we removed it with the tractor and trailer. When putting the manure into the drills two people were needed on the trailer and one on the tractor. The manure was put in grapefulls at regular intervals in each drill. Six drills could be done at one time, two on either side of the trailer and two behind where the wheels of the trailer ran. When the whole field was completed the small heaps were scattered evenly with the grape along each drill before the potatoes were dropped and the light sprinkling of potash sown.

The remainder of the dunghill was spread on the grass fields, this time "broadcast" from the trailer. In the case of a field of lea which was going to be ploughed for corn, the manure would be spread fairly heavily on the surface and then ploughed down. The dunghill would eventually be completely cleared with the last vestiges of manure swept clean. It was always strange to see the vacant space again, with the entrance into the haggard open and free once more.

In addition to the normal crops nearly everyone set a vegetable garden. In our own case we grew quite a range of stuff, enough to keep the house going for most of the year. We would have cabbages, lettuce and onions; carrots, turnips and beetroot; radishes, celery, parsley and leeks, together with peas and beans.

It strikes me now as I write that most of the farmhouses at that time were very close indeed to being self-sufficient. The amount of stuff bought in the shops was really quite small. For example we had our own milk, butter, potatoes, vegetables, bread, eggs, and chicken. My mother would normally go to Newry on market day, on a Thursday, and she would bring home chops, or bacon, or very occasionally steak. The butcher's van called each Saturday and meat was bought for the Sunday dinner. For the rest of the week excellent dinners could be provided from our own produce, and, if pushed, the same could have applied to Thursday and Sunday as well. This was produce that was always fresh, pure, and free from all contaminants of any kind.

That situation has now completely changed. All the above produce is bought today in the shops by country dwellers, everything neatly packed, "uniformed" in size, dyed to the appropriate colour, polluted to the appropriate taste.

I have to say that I have smiled to myself often with a sense of irony in recent years as I have listened to newly-enlightened experts extolling the efficacy of this, apparently recently discovered, revolutionary system, which they call Organic Farming. It is almost as if they have invented it. It is simply farming as it always was before industrialists, scientists, and the large corporations got involved. It simply proves once more, as in the case of numerous other aspects of life, that the older generation did, in fact, know best.

Pig Killing

During my childhood in Lislea pig killing was a natural part of the rural way of life. Virtually every small farmer kept pigs. Each would have at least one sow which would produce a new litter of suckers approximately every eight to nine months. One of our more onerous tasks as children was to bring the sow to be serviced at the appropriate time. Since there was no other means of conveyance we had to walk her there and back.

The nearest boar was at Michael John Toal's, some two and a half miles away, most of which was along the main Newry road. It was a long and laborious task. It was fairly tolerable going down but the journey home was often a nightmare. The sow's feet, which were not used to walking on the hard road surface, would be getting sore, the sow herself would be getting tired, and the ardour which she felt on the outward journey would be fading fast. The result would be that she would simply lie down on the side of the road and refuse to budge. There was no point in trying to lift her, and she could not be coaxed. There was no alternative but to stand and wait until the spirit moved her again, and try to hide our embarrassment as best we could at the spectacle we presented to the cars and buses that passed in what seemed a never-ending flow along the main road.

When the suckers were ten to twelve weeks old most farmers sold them, taking them to Camlough, or Newry, market by horse and cart. However, there would nearly always be one or two that would be slightly smaller than the rest and, rather than spoil the evenness of the litter, these would be kept back and fattened for killing. There would also be occasions where a sow had more suckers than she could rear and, consequently, some would have to be reared by hand. These were nearly always kept for fattening. There was always of course "the runt", the smallest pig in the litter, which could hardly ever be sold in the market. Having one or two pigs around a house was useful as they could be fed mostly on the household leftovers, which made their upkeep very cheap.

There were also a number of farmers, including ourselves, who on occasions kept the whole litter, especially if the price for suckers was bad, and fattened them for slaughter. When they reached the appropriate size the females, or "gilts" as they were called, were normally removed and either kept, or sold on, for breeding. The rest continued the fattening process. For whatever reason, there was scarcely a week that someone wouldn't have pigs to be slaughtered somewhere in the area.

At that time there was no such thing as slaughterhouses. All pig killing had to be done at home. This meant that the local slaughter man, "Mickey the Butcher", did a fairly brisk trade throughout most of the year. The day for the pig killing would always be chosen in consultation with him, so as to fit into his schedule.

The morning of the pig killing started early and always had a sense of excitement about it. On rising, a large, three-legged pot would be filled with water and hung from the crook over the open fire to boil. The butcher would normally arrive between eight thirty and nine, carrying his surgical instruments with him, neatly wrapped in a brown jute bag.

Prior to his arrival the site for the killing would have to be prepared. Two steel barrels were taken out into the yard and placed upside down, in our case beside the steps leading to the loft. The stable door was removed and placed lengthwise on top of them. It was then washed down and scrubbed. A rope with a noose at one end was placed on the door. A heavy bedding of fresh, clean straw was spread on the ground beside the barrels. A sledgehammer was left standing nearby. It was time for the proceedings to commence.

The rope was taken in one hand into the pig house and the noose, well slackened, was slipped carefully into the mouth of the first pig, and up around its top jaw. This was done in such a way that the pig did not know what was happening until it felt the noose tighten. It was then too late. At this stage the rope was merely to ensure that the pig could not escape. No pressure was put on it, or the pig would have instinctively pulled backwards making it extremely difficult to get it outside. Instead, someone went behind and caught it by the tail and steered it gently out through the door into the yard. From here it would be pushed forward slowly as it picked its way across the stony ground to the safety of the fresh straw bedding. The pushing now stopped and the rope was tightened. The pig automatically pulled backwards with all its strength against the rope, with its head raised. Of all the pigs I have seen slaughtered not one ever departed from this norm. This instinctive reaction exposed the pig's head as a perfect target. At this stage it squealed continuously and at a pitch that was deafening. On pig-killing day on any farm the squeals could be heard the full length of the valley. The butcher now raised the sledgehammer in the air just above the crown of the squealing pig. As the hammer came down in a fast, well-aimed stroke the squealing stopped abruptly in a stunning silence, as the pig hit the straw, legs under, and lay motionless.

The butcher swiftly took his long, wide-bladed knife and made a deft, straight incision the full length of the pig's throat, from the under jaw to the breastbone. He followed this with two more, deeper, incisions until the sides of the throat fell away like parting lips. This was followed by one sharp inward plunge of the knife to the full extent of the blade, over the breastbone and into the heart. Only now did the blood start to flow.

It was always the task of the woman of the house to catch the blood. She would be standing prepared with a broad tin-dish in her hand. As soon as the butcher had delivered the coup de gras she would quickly insert the rim of the dish under the bottom lip of the throat and collect the blood as it pumped out freely.

This would be used later, mixed with herbs and an assortment of different ingredients, to produce black pudding, a favourite of all the household. This was normally cooked in a tin can and kept in cold storage in the milk house. Depending on the number of pigs to be killed, there would often be enough to last for quite some time.

The pig carcass was now lifted up onto the door and stretched out full length on one side. The cauldron of boiling water was taken out from the kitchen. Its contents were poured slowly, using a small pot or ladle, along the upturned side of the carcass until it was completely soaked and steaming. The butcher would then take a wide-bladed scraper with a short handle and proceed to scrape all the hair and dirt from the carcass. This instrument was very sharp. When he was finished the side would be as smooth as a newly shaved face, with the red sheen of the bacon showing through the skin. The carcass would then be turned over and the same procedure followed on the other side.

When all the scraping was completed it would be time to hang the carcass. To do this the butcher lanced the heel on each back leg to reveal the heel tendon. This was extremely strong and more than capable of bearing the full weight of the carcass. A round stick, about two inches in diameter and eighteen inches long, was inserted on either side between the tendon and the heel bone. The carcass was then carried into the stable where this stick was slotted over a hook suspended from the ceiling joist, and the carcass was allowed to hang freely.

The butcher now took a shorter knife and made an incision the full length of the carcass, from just in front of the back legs down to the breastbone, revealing the internal organs. The heart and liver, which were highly prized as table delicacies, were removed and placed in a bucket of clean water. Next, the layer of fat that was intertwined with the organs would be incised away with surgical precision and placed in the bucket also. At a time before the availability of manufactured cooking fats this was highly prized. It would be used as rendering for frying or roasting.

There was now only one other organ of note to be saved, the one most highly prized by us children, the bladder. Indeed, it was for this alone that we always looked forward to the pig killing. When left to dry for a few hours, the bladder could be blown up, either by mouth or with a bicycle pump, and tied tightly at the neck to form an excellent football. When we were young this was virtually the only type of football we ever had and to us the high pierced squealing of a pig was often a welcome sound!

The rest of the internal organs were removed and thrown to one side, to be buried later in the dunghill. The butcher now took the original knife and, with the help of his wooden mallet, he hammered it through the short remaining distance of the breastbone, to join the incision up with the one already made in the throat. Double-pointed sticks of appropriate decreasing length were inserted crossways at intervals in each side of the stomach flaps down the full length of the carcass, including a short vertical one in the mouth. This allowed the carcass to dry out completely. Finally, the inside was washed down thoroughly with clean cold water. One killing was now complete.

The door was rescrubbed, additional fresh straw put on top of the original, and the same procedure carried out for each successive pig.

The finished carcases were taken to the bacon centre in Newry. In our case my father would bring them on the trailer and tractor, securely wrapped in white linen sheets. I remember on one occasion he had a full trailer load, a line of carcases placed along each side.

Throughout my early life none of the bacon was ever kept for home consumption. There was clear evidence, however, that this was not always the case. In our house, as in the case of many farmhouses in the area, there was a line of short, thick, iron hooks attached to the ceiling of what was then called the kitchen. The sole purpose of these was for hanging cuts of bacon, home-cured and smoked. My father remembered the time when the hooks were in common use, especially during periods of some affluence.

It would appear, however, that these periods may well have been few and far between for some people and that the hooks were very often bare! This is testified to by a story told by my wife's aunt, Mary Ellen Murphy, who was born in Carricknagavna, a town land on the other side of the hill from us. She later became a nun and spent most of her adult life in Canada. On her visits home she often told us stories of her childhood. On one occasion she spoke of her time at school in Newry. At break time some of the more affluent pupils would be discussing what they were going to have for dinner that evening, some saying that they were going to have potatoes and steak, others potatoes and roast beef, and others potatoes and lamb etc. When her turn came Mary Ellen would reply that she was going to have potatoes and Point.

Perhaps because it sounded slightly exotic, no one ever asked her what this was. She explained to us that it was very simple. Coming from a fairly large family as she did, at a time when life was very tight for most people in the countryside, food would often be very sparse. At dinnertime when she and the other children were eating their potatoes and salt they would stick their fork in a piece of potato and point it up towards the hook where the bacon used to be before putting it in their mouth and eating it.

THE KILLING

Gently coaxed
To morning light
She nosed her way
Into the yard.
With ancient scents
Her nostrils twitched,
Her head she raised
With joy,
But held by us
By ear and tail
Beneath the open sky.
Mouth-noose slack
She picked her way
By whitewashed wall and stile
Until she reached the straw-bed laid,
The place where she would die.

Quick snap of rope
And jerk of head
Her heels dug deep into the ground,
The tug-of-war was short and fierce
Her screams a thousand cries.
The hammer blow
Fell swift and sure
Upon her naked crown
In thud of silence
Dropping her
Upon the cushioning pile.

Swift sweep of knife
Down outstretched throat
Into the heart
And she was meat,
Her lifeblood pumped
In fitful bursts
In tin dish caught for family use.

With expert care
Her carcass washed,
Shaved and scraped
Till bacon fresh,
By tendons raised
On cart house hook
The refuse of her organs stripped,
In joints she hung,
In bacon ribs
And gammon steaks,
And pork chops spread
In neat array
On far off shelves.

A change of Destiny

(Higher Education in the 1950's)

Our generation was one of the first to avail of the Eleven Plus system, which was introduced in 1947. This opened the door to Grammar School education for the first time to all, both rich and poor. Previous to this scarcely any children from the small farming communities of South Armagh could afford such an education. Their destiny was to serve their compulsory term in the rural schools and then move onto the land or into trades. But now the Eleven Plus marked a watershed in this hitherto fixed destiny, opening doors that had previously been closed, and allowing the less privileged to cross the social demarcation line. It took some time for this new realisation to sink in, and the number taking advantage of it by my time was still relatively small. In my own case my mother was the driving force.

Being the eldest in her family she was forced in the late 1920's, like so many others of her generation, to emigrate to America, when barely out of her teens, to try and earn money to pay off the mounting debts at home. During her years there she became increasingly aware of the importance of education in the world of advancement. She herself had to make do with the rudimentary knowledge acquired in Lislea National School and she was determined that her children should have more. When the Eleven Plus system was introduced she immediately set her sights on it. In 1949 she removed my older brother, Joe, from Lislea School and got him into the Abbey Christian Brothers' Primary School in Newry where he would have a chance to do the exam. He passed and moved into the Grammar School.

In 1951 my turn came, much against my own wishes and despite my many protestations. Almost eleven years of age, I was already scenting the green fields and open spaces that beckoned three years hence. My only wish then was to get onto the farm fulltime. It was with it that my affinity lay, ever since early childhood. My mother, however, would have none of it. She headed off once more into the Abbey to try to get her second son accepted. Since the first stage of the Eleven Plus exam was only a couple of months away, and because of the large numbers in the classes already, she was told that I would have to do an entrance test before I would be accepted.

I still remember vividly walking into Pete Curran's R.I.P. class on the day of that test, with my overcoat, which I was fast outgrowing, pulled tightly around my waist and fastened with one button. I was confronted with a sea of faces, thirty-two pupils packed into one room, almost as many as there were in the whole of Lislea School at the time. There was a small table and chair placed in the corner at the top of the room. I was put sitting there and Mr. Curran placed an examination paper before me, one of the previous years' tests. I have no recollection whatsoever of what was on it or how well I might have done. When the time was up Mr. Curran took the paper and went through it. He then called my mother who had been seated out in the hallway and told her that he would take me in.

My next dreaded task was to ask the master in Lislea School for a transfer. It was with shaking legs that I approached his table, not to "ask out" for a day this time, but forever. After initial surprise on his part, followed by much questioning and clear dissatisfaction, he finally produced the transfer form, filled it in, and signed it. I took it from him, picked up my bag and walked out through the door for the last time, out to a changed destiny.

Moving from the small confines of Lislea School into the much more complex structure of the Abbey, which contained over six hundred pupils, was a major cultural shock. This was added to the following year when, having passed the Eleven Plus, I moved down the hill to the Abbey Grammar School. Here I was introduced for the first time to Irish, together with a wide range of other subjects, many of which I had scarcely ever heard of before, such as French, Science, Latin, along with more advanced forms of mathematics such as Algebra and Trigonometry. My favourite subject from the start was Irish. I had an immediate affinity with it, without knowing why. Through the years I came to realise that it was the language that spoke most directly of my people, a receptacle of the values and traditions from which we had sprung.

In the mid 1950's higher education was still something of a novelty in Lislea. The tradition of pupils leaving school at the earliest possible opportunity that the law would allow was still prevalent and, as I have said in other places, I watched many of them, with a great sense of envy, as they kicked their school bags up the road before them with sheer delight on the last day of their imprisonment. Leaving school marked a kind of coming-of-age. It was only then that the traditional short trousers, always worn at school, were discarded and long trousers were worn for the first time. These marked the entry into adulthood. But now that tradition was slowly changing.

For the older people, especially, it was puzzling to see students who were almost young men, sporting long trousers, and still at school. In their own childhood, before compulsory schooling was introduced, education was much more of an optional affair. Each year was marked by a different book, so that the number of books each had done indicated the number of years he, or she, had spent at school.

I was never able to find out exactly what these "books" consisted of, but it would appear that they were a grinding in the basics of language and numeracy. It was clear, however, that each book represented a distinct, and unquestioned, demarcation line between the various levels of educational achievement and, hence, ability.

You would often hear people in the Céilí house asking each other what book they had left school in. You would also hear someone saying that he had to leave school in the second book to go out to be hired; or, if the conversation was about someone who had done very well in life, you might hear someone saying that it was a credit to him and "him that left school in the fourth book". The highest accolade of all was reserved for those few who had reached the pinnacle of academic achievement, those who had gone on to do the seventh, and last, book. Their position was normally unassailable.

I remember one occasion, when I was preparing for the Senior Examination, the equivalent of modern day G.C.S.E., going down to the Mall in Newry with all my mates to catch the bus home. There was an old gentleman there, one of the older members of the Lislea community, and I went up and stood beside him. He looked at the bag on my back and said,

"You're not still at school, are you?" When I told him that I was he looked at me with surprise and said, "Shur, you "beeda have" (i.e. must have) all the books done by now! What book are you in at the minute?"

There was I standing with a bag bulging with books, all the textbooks covering the whole range of subjects I was doing, enough almost to fill a wheelbarrow. I realised that, short of giving him a complete indoctrination into the whole new educational system, which he would most likely not have understood, there was no answer I could give him.

This was the first time that I became aware of a gulf that was now opening between the older generation and the new one, which I and my kind represented. This man could not even have begun to understand what was involved in this new age of learning, nor, I doubt, could he have been convinced of its necessity.

This sense of estrangement was to increase considerably the following year when, after doing A Level, I qualified for University. Prior to this, although some students in the previous few years with the aid of the Eleven Plus system had gone to Training College, no one from Lislea had gone to University. In that year, 1959, a local lad and myself were the first two setting out.

During the months of summer prior to leaving, as I worked on the farm, I began to question the efficacy of the whole business. It seemed to me that this higher education affair was getting out of hand. It was against all the traditions that I had known for young people from a small country area like Lislea, who had been born and reared in the time-honoured rural tradition and who had worked since childhood in field, byre, and haggard, to be entertaining the idea of heading off to the lofty heights of University Education. It was to me a paradox, and one that weighed heavily on my mind.

The uncertainty I felt was added to by the fact that, since there was no precedent, there was no path marked out for us to follow. We were heading off into what was uncharted territory. I felt that once I set out I would be leaving home, both literally and metaphorically, perhaps for good.

To me University Education had always seemed to be on a higher, distant plain, trod only by those who were following a pre-laid path that led out from the privilege of birth and heritage. It involved a quest for deeper knowledge and for higher truths, for philosophies of life and for certainties; for all the things that had never formed any part of life in the windswept hills and mountains of South Armagh. For the first time in my life my background now seemed to be my obstacle.

Life in Belfast was completely different to the life in any of the small rural communities of South Armagh. Not only was it vast in comparison, but there seemed to be people everywhere, pouring down every street and side avenue. But these were people who always seemed to be in a hurry. Nowhere would you hear a friendly greeting, nor would you see people stopping for a chat. Life here seemed to be almost impersonal. I managed to get digs with Mrs McCullough, at 41 Tate's Avenue, a place where I was destined to spend four very happy years; but throughout that time I never got to know who lived on either side of me. This was something that could never have happened at home.

Queen's University at that time was quite an imposing place. Its tall graceful buildings and elegant archways lent it a sense of reverence and antiquity. You could not help but think of all the learned men of the past who had graced its cloisters. It was still, however, very much the preserve of the elite. Although there was a significant intake that year of students like myself, the sons of small farmers, labourers, bakers etc., from many areas throughout the North, we were still very much in the minority. We seemed, indeed, to be an object of some interest to the sophisticates who walked the campus. Initially, when asked where I was from, I would reply "from Lislea". On seeing the look of puzzlement on the face of the enquirer I would explain that it was a small country area not far from Newry. I would then get the reply, "Oh yes — Right — Golly good!" Eventually I would simply reply "from beside Newry."

First year students at University were called "Freshers". They stood out from the rest because of a certain gaucheness, due to their inexperience. I was determined not to be taken as one of these. I adopted an air of confident nonchalance as I groped my way from place to place and started to practise a new, more polished, accent as fast as I could. All traces of my rural background, and heritage, had to be disguised as quickly as possible in these hallowed hallways of high learning. I would subconsciously be looking down at my shoes to make sure that there was no cow dung still clinging to them.

As I envisaged, the quest for broader meanings and deeper truths was a major feature of university life, both formally and informally. This was a process to which I had already been introduced, but to a much smaller degree, at A Level. Once you passed the stage of G.C.S.E., education took on a new dimension. No longer was it sufficient to amass facts and figures to be regurgitated at a later date. Education now called for exploration, assessment, personal opinion. There were no set, neat answers any more. You were forced to seek your own definition, your own truth.

This process was accelerated greatly at university. The only problem was that the more informal discussions I had, the more books I read, and the more lectures I attended, the more elusive this truth seemed to become. All that I had taken for granted before was thrown into the melting pot and, instead of a definitive truth, all I was acquiring was a growing uncertainty. At each turn there were tangential pathways that led not to answers but to more questions, and new aspects of truth, which added to the diversity and uncertainty that I had already accumulated. Each of these pathways seemed to be leading me farther and farther from home. What I was seeking was some type of singular truth, a truth that would have a universality that would apply to all men in all ages. As I looked for it in academic tomes, on high shelves of learning, and down laneways of abstract thought the more elusive it became.

First year students were divided into groups and each group was allocated a professor who acted as an advisory tutor. The idea was, I think, that if anyone encountered a major problem on which he needed advice he could go to his personal tutor, although I never knew of anyone who did. The tutor would hold a meeting with the group as a whole about three times a year for an informal chat and discussion. The turn of my group, which also contained my fellow countryman came towards the end of the first term. By now my new accent had come on quite well, to the extent that I felt reasonably assured that I could be mistaken for a member of the cognoscenti. This illusion was to be suddenly, and very rudely, shattered!

When I entered the meeting room people were milling around. It was a very informal affair, with coffee served and the professor lying back on his chair smoking his pipe. The great shock was that everywhere I turned all I could hear were Oxford and Cambridge accents. Their beautifully crafted tonal rhythms filled the room as their owners moved with grace and ease amongst the group. They had a suavity that matched their language, both of which were inbred and gave them an immediate sense of distinction and superiority. My jaw dropped immediately and I became almost tongue-tied. How could I ever hope to compete with people like these? Never before had I felt so out of place in any room! I took my cup of coffee and tried to remain as far as I could in the one spot so that I would have to speak as little as possible. I knew immediately that my freshly polished accent wouldn't stand a chance here!

After the informalities were over and everyone was seated the professor introduced a topic of conversation, mostly to break the ice and get people speaking. The topic he chose, perhaps quite deliberately, was the well-known poem by Wordsworth, "Ode on the Intimations of Immortality". He set out to explore the central meaning of the poem and to try and identify the particular point of truth the poet was trying to establish.

The discussion started a little slowly at first but quickly gathered pace. It was soon in full flow and becoming increasingly more interesting. Opinions were being batted to and fro as the professor gently steered them towards the core issue. It was quite some time before I realised, to my great surprise, that the only people in the room who were speaking were my friend and myself. Despite the professor's best efforts, at times almost to the point of embarrassment, the posh accents remained totally silent. He could not rouse a single opinion from one of them as their owners sat with a look of uncomfortable bewilderment on their faces.

Wordsworth's poem dealt with his changing relationship with nature and with his own environment. In childhood he had had an instinctive affinity with everything around him. He would run joyfully through the hills and dales, and along upland streams, feeling at one with them. This bond was completely uninhibited, and more importantly, unquestioned. As he grew older he began to feel a growing sense of despair as this natural, unthinking rapport began to fade. Eventually he felt completely cut off from it. The poem ends with his sense of joy as he rediscovers it again in adulthood, but this time on a more cognitive and objective level. He could see now, and appreciate more fully, the beauty, peace, and untarnished truth with which he had communed instinctively as a child. He had rediscovered his environment and his heritage. In so doing he had rediscovered himself, his own truth.

In discussing this my friend and I were merely speaking of our own life, the life that we had known since childhood in South Armagh. Wordsworth's poem might as well have been set there as in his homeland in the Lake District. In this regard we had an expertise which the rest lacked. I suddenly realised that knowledge was not the preserve of any one group of people, nor was education. They both dealt with life's reality, not with pretension, or with abstract idealism. Here we were in one of the hallowed rooms of Belfast's University, with a distinguished professor trying to carve a path to the timeless truth that lies at the heart of rock and stone, the very things that I had been trying to deny!

I suddenly realised, with a shock of surprise, that the truth which I had been seeking in distant places was where I had left it and where it had always been, in the hills, mountains, and quarried fields of South Armagh, and in the people who inhabited them. These were a people who had no need to rediscover the truth of themselves, because they had never lost it. Theirs was a constancy of existence, and of truth. They had lived at one with their environment and with nature from the beginning of time, communing instinctively on a daily basis not only with its beauty but also with its demands and its timeless challenge. They were guided by basic values that had been handed down through countless generations. It was there that my own truth lay.

That day I found what the great Gaelic poet, Mairtín O Direáin from the Aran Islands, called his "Cranna Foirtil", his "Beams of Strength". I knew that henceforth, no matter where I went or what I did, I would be supported by these beams of strength, provided I remained true to them. If I didn't, everything I would do would be false.

I immediately stripped away the new affectation of speech and re-honed the edges of my South Armagh accent to their original sharp point of purity.

Henceforth no place, or no people, would ever again cause me to stand in awe! From that point on, metaphorically speaking, I sought out every patch of cow dung I could find and danced in it with exultation!

LEARNING

I have walked from mountains where
Wild heather stored the sun
And bluebells raced the hills before
The springtime bracken came,

To cities where the masses flowed
In rivers of dry stone,
No distant sound of laughter heard
Where rocks greet mountain streams.

And I have stood and watched them pass,
The hill clay on my shoes,
No moon-soft bracken adding grace,
No smile of hawthorn bloom.

And I have walked their hallways where
Professors in posh tones
Spoke of truth of life and odes
Carved straight from mountain stone.

And I determined then to take
These hillsides where I'd go,
To all the classrooms I would walk,
The hill clay on my shoes.

And I have quarried them with words,
The chisel of my trade,
And left on blackboards outlined trace
Of rock and hill and stone.

And I have heard wise students speak
In posh tones they have won
Of all that they have learned now
Of hill and rock and stone.

The Decline of the Irish Language in Lislea.

Some years ago I came across a document which contained significant information concerning the status of Irish in Lislea in the early 1830's. It was brought to my attention by a fellow past pupil of the Abbey. Where he got it from I do not know.

This document was written in the year 1925 by a man called Nugent, a Gaelic scholar of the period and a schoolteacher, and was still in its original manuscript form. Amongst other information it stated that in the year 1833, (the year in which the first "National" School was opened in Lislea,) Irish was spoken as widely in this area as it then was (i.e. in 1925) in Rannafast.

As most people know, Rannafast was, and still is, the dominant Gaelic speaking area in the North. When I myself first began to frequent this part of Donegal in the late 1950's it would be very seldom that one would hear a word of English there. This would have been much more so the case in 1925.

Allowing for even a very large amount of exaggeration on the part of the writer, this is still a very striking claim and it would suggest that when Lislea National School was first opened the language that would have been carried through its doors would have been predominantly Irish.

That situation was to change utterly before the end of that same century, due in some part, perhaps, to the system of National School education itself, but much more so to the very traumatic years that were soon to follow, the years of famine, emigration and mass extinction that started in the mid 1840's which were destined to have such a devastating effect on the social, economic and cultural history of Ireland as a whole.

A clear sign of this effect in Lislea can be seen in the demographic changes in the area after this traumatic period. As revealed by Mr T. Keane in his book "Lislea Church And Community", the number of children of school-going age in Lislea in the year 1831 was estimated at 200. Just thirty years later, in 1861, this number had dropped to "100 or less". Equally revealing, as regards the changes in the financial fortunes of the people, is the fact that, since a small school fee had to be paid, the actual average number of pupils attending the school "was a mere 30!"

It would appear that the decline of the Irish language in this area, as in most other areas throughout South Armagh, matched these significant demographic changes. My own father R.I.P. was born in the year 1897 and he knew only three people in the Lislea area who could speak Irish, only one of whom, Sally Humphreys, was a native speaker. The language had been almost completely wiped out in Lislea in the space of some sixty years.

A hundred years prior to this such a linguistic change would have been unimaginable. During the eighteenth century, the last great Gaelic literary age in Ireland, normally referred to as the golden age of Irish literature, virtually all the major poets of Ulster came from the South East Ulster area, and predominantly from the South Armagh/North Louth region, the territory traditionally known as the Fews; men such as Peadar Ó Doirnín, Pádraig Mc Alinden, Art McCooey, Séamas Dall Mac Cuarta.

In addition to these there were a host of lesser poets such as Randal Dall Mac Dónaill, Fergus Mac a' Bheatha, Séamas Mac GiollaChoille, Muiris Ó Gormáin, etc etc. As a result, this area was referred to as Ceantar Na bhFilí, the land of the poets, and also Ceantar Na n-Amhrán, the land of the songs. Whatever changes might take place in other areas one would have assumed that South Armagh would have been the last to forego its outstanding linguistic tradition. This, however, was not to be. Within a hundred years of the death of Art McCooey in 1773, the last of these major poets, the Irish Language had virtually ceased to exist.

In many ways this great change was mirrored in the life of Sally Humphreys herself. When she was born in Levelamore in the first half of the nineteenth century, into a family called Mc Glade, Irish was the language of her household, as it was of the other households around her. It was her natural mode of expression, something she would never have given any thought to. However, she lived long enough to see this change utterly, until in the years before her death she came to occupy the unenviable position of being the last native Irish speaker in the area, an object of curiosity and of some interest.

Sally Humphries had been a noted Gaelic singer and she had a large repertoire of songs and airs, especially those from the eighteenth century. As a result her house was visited often by song collectors and by a new breed of young Irish scholars who had started to take an interest in the language.

Ironically, perhaps, this house in which she spent her married life had formerly been occupied by the famous Gaelic Bishop, Dr. Pádraig Ó Donnghaile, whose memory is enshrined in the song The Bard of Armagh.

Sally Humphreys, died in 1918, some twenty odd years before I was born, and with her died a linguistic tradition in Lislea which, subject only to its own natural changes, had stretched back in an unbroken line to the dawn of history.

LASMUIGH DE THEACH SHORCHA

Is minic mé anseo os comhair do thí
Daichead bliain ó shin, ar thaobh na gcianta
De do ghuth, agus na línte filíochta úd
Á n-aithris agat do lucht an tsiúil

Is déistean id' ghlór don leagan Béarla úr
A d'iompair siadsan leo, nár thug leis trasna
Ach rabhcán an phróis ó amhrán do mhuintire.

Is mairg gan mé sa tsiúl iarnóin sin na nduan
Faoi mhaidhm do ghutha anseo ag an fhoinse
s fuarán ár sinsear ag sileadh trí do bhriathra,

Is chuirfinn do ghlór i dtaisce in idhre m'intinne
Is bheadh agam treoir maidin earraigh seaca
Is mé ar an éagmais seasta lasmuigh de do theachsa
Ag iarraidh eochair chasta a chur i nglas mo thosta.

Gan fágtha ansin romham ach ballóg liath do theanga,
Gan fágtha de d'amhrán ach curfá fann i mbriathra
A shíob mar shiorradh gaoithe trí chanúint mo dhaoine.
Gan de chaidreamh agam feasta le do dhúchas ná do smaointe
Ach comhfhuaim sin na mblianta ina rithimí gaothscríte
As a sníomhfainn friotal a d'oirfeadh do mo laethe,
Lena gcuirfinn forán ar na bánta is na sléibhte,
Mé im' aonar seasta ag sníomh cheirtlín gaoithe.

SALLY HUMPHREYS

Often I have stood here before your house
Forty years ago on the leeside of your voice
As you sang your song to the worshipers
Who had come bearing gifts of verse
From a foreign tongue to incense your mind
With pride of place and heritage as you sang
The obsequies of your race, with disdain in your voice
For the raucous prose their version brought
From the bright rippling streams of your origins
Where your voice sourced deep in the limpid spring
Of your Gaelic past.

My great regret that I missed
The twilight of our song, as it fell
In the dying cascade of your words
So that the aimed current
Of your voice might have scored
In the target of my mind,
As well as heart,

As I stood here before your house
On your threshold of neglect
On a cold morning in spring
Trying to turn a twisted key
In the lock of our silence.

Nothing then before me
But the grey ruins of your tongue
Nothing of your song but assonance of years
Threading its refrain through my people's words,
Nothing of your time or your heritage
From which I might weave a language for our days,
With which I might hail the wasteland and the hills
As I stood alone weaving rhythms from the wind.

Calmor's Rock

Calmor's Rock is situated opposite Topny Mountain, at the north entrance to the western valley of the Ring of Gullion. I was born just a short distance down the road from it and my friends and I spent many hours around the rock as children. With its high secluding hedge and adjoining copse of trees it provided numerous nooks and crannies which were ideal for many different children's games especially Tig and Hide-and-Seek.

In addition to this there was a small cave at the top of the rock which was always a source of temptation. The climb up the face was not only arduous but also quite dangerous as the only grip you had were the tufts of grass sticking out from the ledges. The climb, however, was always worth it. When you reached the cave you felt on top of the world. Although not very big, it was surprisingly larger than it appeared from the road below. There was sufficient room for two people to move back into it out of sight. Further progress was prevented by two large stones, the points of which were sunk down into the cave floor. They had all the appearance of having fallen down at some period in the past blocking off what would appear to have been a much bigger cave.

To us, who had been taught absolutely nothing at school about our own environment, or our history, this, like many other landmarks in the Ring of Gullion, was just an ordinary place, a rock around which we could play our childhood games. It was many years before I learned the truth about the rock.

In the early 1960's I was engaged in a thesis, which was part of a Post-Graduate course at Queen's University. I was doing my research in the Stack, the reference section of Queen's University Library. The "Stack" was a very appropriate name for this area, since that is exactly what it was, a voluminous pile of books stacked up in layers from the floor to the vaulted ceiling. A narrow iron staircase led up from one level to the next. On each level there were facilities for reading and taking notes.

The Stack was a place where time stood still. Hours would fly by virtually unnoticed. On all sides you were surrounded by books, as far as you could see, many of them very old. This gave the whole place an ambience of both learning and antiquity. The biggest problem always was to stick to the subject in hand. Each book you pulled out, although perhaps not relevant to your topic, would have something in it which would catch your eye and force you to sit down and read it. As regards the thesis that I was supposed to be researching, many an evening was wasted in this way. On one such occasion I pulled out a book dealing with historic events in the seventeenth century and opened it at random.

My eye was immediately caught by a story which fascinated me. Before me was an account of a notorious raparee of the latter half of the seventeenth and the beginning of the eighteenth century. It said he was born in the town land of Dorsey, which was only a few miles up the road from where I was born, and that he headed a band of bloodthirsty villains who spread terror in both planters and natives alike. Before anyone was allowed into his band he had to supply proof that he had killed at least one man. The account went on to say that his name was Cathal Mór Ó Carrachóir and that he had many hideouts in South Armagh but that the one he frequented most was in a small town land called Lislea, beside a rock which still bore his name!

This was the first time that I had ever seen Lislea mentioned in a book, especially an important historical reference book in a place of high learning. Until then I had always imagined that history had passed Lislea by. The reference to "the rock which still bore his name" began to race through my mind — Cathal Mór? — Cal Mór — Calmor's Rock!

My amazement was indeed great. The simple rock around which I had played as a child was now completely transformed in my mind. Although Cathal Mór may not have had the historical pedigree that one would have wished, at least he had a history, and a place worthy of mention in the annals of the past. To someone who had succeeded in being educated, down all the pathways of supposed high learning, with a complete ignorance of his own history this was very significant indeed. This was my road to Damascus!

From here on this rock would stand as a symbol to me. The cave in its forehead was like a door leading into another world, a world of which I had been completely ignorant. I was destined to be drawn through this door and into this world, a world of legends, romance, poetry, song, a world of history, mythology and larger-than-life figures, of heroic deeds, brigands, saints, and timeless scholars, — the colourful polyglot that forms the unique cultural landscape of the Ring of Gullion.

The life story of Cathal Mór was quite indicative of his era. He was a first generation descendant of the landed gentry whose father had lost all his possessions in the Cromwellian confiscations. This quite clearly embittered Cathal to such an extent that he turned his family's long military tradition into a campaign of havoc and vengeance, wrecking both indiscriminately. He followed the lifestyle which he felt was due to him from birth, always dressing in the finest clothes, topped off with a long flowing wig, a dandy in fact.

Although raparee-hunting was quite a major business at the time, the head of each raparee fetching five pounds, a considerable amount of money then, Cathal Mór avoided all attempts at capture. He was more than a match for these relatively amateurish pursuers.

It wasn't until the arrival of John Johnston, or "Johnston of the Fews" as he was known, that he was put under any great pressure. The term "Fews" comes from the Irish word "feadha" meaning trees, and refers essentially to the territory covered by the extensive wood of Dunreavey, which at one time stretched from Crossmaglen down to the outskirts of Newry.

Johnston, a lessee landlord, was appointed Constable of the Fews in 1710, with the particular brief of ridding the area of Raparees, or Tories as they were then called.

History has not been kind to Johnston. He comes down almost as a dark shadow hanging over the Fews. Both guilty and innocent were subject equally to his wrath. The poets especially came in for particular attention. Being the only educated people of the peasant class, whose poetry acted as a mouthpiece for their grievances, they were constantly under suspicion of sedition and were very often forced to go on the run. This applied especially to Art McCooey, Peadar Ó Doirnín, and the legendary poet-cum-raparee Séamas Mór Mc Murphy. Indeed, it was while hiding out from

Johnston in Creggan graveyard that McCooey wrote his most famous poem, ÚrChill a' Chreagáin (The Beautiful Churchyard of Creggan), which was destined to become the most popular song of the area for over a hundred and fifty years, almost the National Anthem of South East Ulster.

As the law stood at the time anyone apprehended by a Government agent whom they suspected of being a raparee could be legally beheaded, without any further proof being required. Johnston's chief lieutenant was a man called Keenan who seems to have taken a particular delight in applying this law rigorously. As a result he earned for himself the nickname "Caonán na gCeann", or "Keenan of the Heads". It is estimated that he personally beheaded approximately 110 people in the Fews area during Johnston's reign.

In the year 1714 Cathal Mór appears on Johnston's list of wanted men, with a reward of twenty pounds on his head. Despite the reward, and despite Johnston's best efforts over the next three years, he failed to capture Cathal Mór. Cathal's activities, if anything, increased during those years until he eventually acquired the status of public enemy number one. In the year 1717 he headed Johnston's list and the reward on him was raised to one hundred pounds, an enormous figure in those days.

In the end Johnston never managed to capture Cathal Mór. The distinction for that was to go to another man. In the latter half of the year 1717 a certain Captain Mervyn Pratt was specially commissioned as Officer-in-Charge of all the Crown militia in the Fews for the purpose of tracking down the most notorious of the Raparees, especially Cathal Mór.

Cathal was finally cornered in a house on the Dundalk to Newtown Hamilton road, not far from Ballsmill, after carrying out another robbery. The house was surrounded and he was apprehended, together with three of his henchmen and his nephew, who was only eighteen years of age. He was put on trial in Dundalk on 17th February 1718 and was sentenced to be hung, drawn and quartered. This sentence was carried out in Dundalk the following day. Cathal Mór made an eloquent, and surprisingly contrite, speech from the gallows, begging forgiveness from all those whom he had injured or in any way wronged and imploring God to forgive him his dark deeds as he entrusted his soul into his keeping.

Three days later his nephew, Patrick Carragher, whose first outing this had been, together with the other three men met the same fate. As was the tradition of the time the four quarters of Cathal Mór's body were each placed at the scenes of his worst atrocities. His head was spiked at Dundalk Gaol, being placed higher than the rest, and still sporting his flowing wig, as a clear warning that even the mightiest would fall.

When the authorities later learned of the existence of the hideout most frequented by him in Lislea, Cathal Mór's head was removed from Dundalk and transferred there where it was placed above the rock which still bears his name, a clear deterrent to others in the area who might be inclined to follow his example.

THE ROCK

The old road
From Dealga Fort to Eamhain Macha
Floats gracefully bedecked in modern
Splendour, almost concealing
Her promiscuous past
Until a wanton gesture, sensuous
Flash of thigh, betrays her origin.

Here where her nipple shows
With sudden twist of corner
Calmor lay. No tar McAdamed frieze,
No gruaibhin frills conceals his
Austere presence, his roar still audible
In the dried throat of jagged stone

And sturdy ash standing sentinel
To his wrath. The eye welcomes
The sudden slit of his staring cave
Set like a jewel in the rock's forehead
Breaking the monotony of refinement,

Hung in a raucous frame
Between the past and now,
Reflecting in its darkening rays
The pain, the ignorance, and the splendour!

Quarrying in Lislea

From my earliest memory Lislea Quarry was one of the main landmarks in our area. An extended face of granite rock, it sits to the left of the main Newry road below Lislea Chapel. In the late 1940's I helped my father on a number of occasions, after he acquired the tractor, to load stones on to the trailer for surfacing the farmyard. At that time the stones were still lying in heaps along the quarry floor and could be easily gathered up with the shovel. It was hard to believe then, and even harder now, that this gaunt, vacant space was once, literally, a hive of activity, with steam-run tractors, lorries, stone crusher, cranes and sett-makers filling the entire area.

At one time, especially during the mid 1920's, Lislea Quarry made a very significant contribution to the welfare of the area. At a time when work was at a premium in most places in Ireland, and virtually impossible to find in England, Lislea Quarry provided fulltime employment for 120 men. That would have represented a very significant proportion of the entire work force of the area. In many cases the only alternative to getting a job in the quarry was the hiring fair.

The quarrying business in Lislea lasted in total for over thirty years. It started off in a small way at the end of the previous century in the persons of the Maginnis brothers, John and Owen, from Amakane. At that time they concentrated on dressed and polished stone for the building trade and for headstones. As their business grew they moved to the large outcrop of basalt rock at the foot of Slieve Gullion, called Carraiganure Rock.

It was here that what would eventually prove to be the main output of the whole Maginnis quarrying enterprise was started, the making of setts, or paving stones. These resembled modern day brick, only sculpted by hand from hard basalt rock. They were almost indestructible due to the hard nature of the stone. This made them immediately popular and the demand for them soon became very great. More men were employed to meet this demand.

The sett-making was a highly skilled trade and brought in many men from the outlying regions, some of them from very far afield, Such as Patrick

Hannaway from Sligo. As it turned out Patrick was destined to remain in the area where he married a local girl and started a very distinguished family dynasty which has made a major contribution to the social and artistic life of Lislea during my lifetime. Lislea setts were used widely in local towns. At one time virtually all the streets in Newry were paved with them. The only place where they remain visible there today is along the Mall. As well as local consumption, there was a large demand for the setts to pave the dockland areas of Belfast, Liverpool and Glasgow.

The setts had to be drawn from Lislea Quarry to Newry by horse and cart. My father was one of the people employed in this work. It was by no means an easy task. The journey was some six miles, with the long, steep hill of Sturgan Brae in between. It took considerable strength and skill to hold back the horse and cart going down this long incline to prevent the horse from slipping, or being forced forward by the weight behind. The driver would have to walk the whole of the inward journey. He would be able to ride in the empty cart on the way home. The price he was paid for each load was two shillings, which in most cases was as much as anyone could manage in a day.

None of the work in the quarry was easy. The face stone had to be bored and split by hand. The large slabs of rock had to be further broken and split into the rough dimensions required by the sett-makers. The stone that was left over, a considerable amount, had to be broken down with twenty-pound sledgehammers into small stone and gravel suitable for road surfacing.

There was one small incident that occurred in the quarry that caused something of a consternation in its time. When some men split a slab of rock in the northern end of the quarry, beside the Ballard road, a large beetle walked out from a pouch-like indentation in the stone. This caused a sense of panic amongst a lot of the men. They took it as some kind of evil omen. It remained a talking point in the area for decades to come. I heard the story often in childhood from different sources, especially during the time of the Céilí house when it still was a cause of wonder. As I grew older I used smile at the quaint imagination of the people before I was born and their naivety at believing such a story.

Ironically, recent scientific and biological research, as I see from a number of programmes on television, have led experts to the belief that such events could actually happen; that insects can be trapped in rock, especially in small pockets inside cooled lava, and survive indefinitely in a form of suspended animation.

That beetle could have been worth a fortune! If anyone had had the courage to catch it, instead of running away from it, we could have been famous forever more, and be known as The Town Land of the Beetle!

Money would now be flooding in from the International Monetary Fund, The European Heritage Fund, The National Lottery, S.A.T.I. and numerous other sources to build a Heritage Centre to house the beetle, and men from the B.B.C. would be coming out in droves to interview us.

However, it was not to be. It wandered off alone up towards Ballard, like "Oisín after the Fianna", into a strange and utterly changed world.

The outbreak of the First World War proved to be a boon to Lislea Quarry. With the absence of imports the demand for the stone, and especially the setts, became even greater. In 1915, with the death of one of the Maginnis brothers, the business was bought by a Belfast Company, Ardle Lupton & Co. They revolutionised the operation by introducing mechanisation into the quarry for the first time. This was in the form of a large steam crane and steam tractors. This was brought a major step forward in 1922 when the quarry once more changed hands. It was taken over by the huge Belfast firm of Charles Tennent & Co. Ltd.

This firm completed the modernisation of the quarry by introducing another crane, both steam and petrol lorries, and erecting a large stone-crushing, or granulating plant, to break down the stone into various grades for road surfacing and for concrete. By this time quarrying in Lislea was at its height. It was now big business.

Anyone who could get employment of any kind in the quarry took it. My uncle, James Mc Parland, when still only a lad, worked there doing odd jobs in the evening after school and at the weekend. There were eight in his family. His father was off in England, very often without work. The financial position at home, as in numerous other households, was precarious. Every shilling that he could earn would make a major difference.

When he was ten years old James was crushed to death between one of the new steam engines and a trailer when, unseen by the driver, he went behind to help with coupling up the trailer. It was an enormous shock to all the family but most especially to his mother Kathryn, who never really got over it. One thing that always stuck in my mind, and still does, was the fact that when they brought his body home a ten-shilling note was found in his pocket. Ten shillings would have been a significant amount of money at that time, especially for a young boy to have earned by himself. I often think of the joy he must have felt when he received his pay that morning and how much he would have been looking forward to going home in the evening to present that note to his mother.

I never knew James except in story. He was spoken of very frequently by many different members of the family. The only name he was ever given was "Wee James". His mother, my grandmother, lived into her ninety first year. She spent many years at the end of her life living with us, being cared for by my mother. Throughout the time I knew her, right up until her death, she would speak frequently of "Wee James". Like the figures on Milton's Grecian Urn he remained forever young, forever fair. Old Kathryn carried the pain of his loss with her throughout her life and into her grave.

IN MEMORIAM- WEE JAMES

Thin wisps of sunlight haunt
The peaks high up,
Dim memory now in the valley
Folding into shadows;
The black fluff of crows
Drifting towards trees
Along ditches and headlands
To the slight rise of quarry,
Pebble and shingle
Caressing the dark.

No blood now upon the stones.

The eternity of peace
Recalls the crushed bones,
Limp body falling
Between tractor and stone
And the interminable pain,
Hushed reminder
In darkened eyes.
Even at ninety she spoke of it
In the back room
Pale face sculptured
In dancing flame.

We all took part
In her ritual sacrifice,
Our youth the altar
For her pain,
At every festive time
Or quiet evening, just like now,
When a sudden guilt
At abandoning him to happiness
Made her don the sack-cloth
Of memory.
She offered him up,
The horror renewed
In the awful simplicity
Of gnarled hands
And rosary beads and soft words
Hammering on our hearts.

Here under the lee of the hill
Where tombstones greet
The coming moon
She lies beside him now
In the growing dusk,

The prison of her heart unlocked,
Whispering softly into shadows.

In 1924 a significant new undertaking was initiated locally when it was decided to pave the main Camlough road from the Egyptian Arch into Newry. The paving was to consist of long sections of concrete separated by asphalt. Lislea Quarry was chosen to supply all the material for the concrete. This was a major order which added greatly to the business in that and the following year. This undertaking would have been quite a novel one at the time when we consider that the rest of the main roads, including the Camlough road itself, were surfaced only with stones and gravel. This concrete paving was to survive for many decades after the advent of tarmacadam. It was there throughout my years as a pupil of the Abbey Grammar School and for many years after I started teaching there. It is only in comparatively recent years that it was resurfaced.

It was only shortly before my father died in 1973 that I learned that no main roads were surfaced as they are now until the 1930's, not all that many years before I was born. It was something that I had never really thought about before. Prior to that time the councils used contract out sections of roadway to local men for maintenance. My father was one such contractor. Their job was to keep the road surface in permanent repair. This meant frequent filling in of the ruts made by wheels, predominantly cart wheels, and the many potholes caused by heavy rain and sinkage. The stone and gravel for this purpose was acquired in Lislea Quarry.

During my childhood and youth, although the main roads were tarmacadamed, none of the rural byroads were surfaced with anything other than stones and grit, and often very little even of that. In our area roads such as The Crooked Road, The Ballard Road, Courtney Road, The Duburren Road, Barr road and numerous others were more like rough tracks than roads. The one that I was most used to, because it was only a short distance from our house and because some of our land was situated on both sides of it, was The Crooked Road. The origin of this name, its official title, becomes immediately obvious once you start to travel it. It is a classic example of a byroad whose layout was dictated entirely by the horse and cart. It runs up through a shallow pass between Lislea Mountain and Burr Mountain, right over the summit and onwards into the town land of Annacloughmullion. As it makes its way up the steep mountain face it follows a twisting horizontal route with many turns. This allowed the hill to be negotiated in short sections, leaving a number of areas where the horse could be rested in safety after a straight pull up a section of the hill. The ground there was comparatively level and there would be no risk of the cart pulling the horse back.

The road surface was like that of all other byroads; two bare parallel strips on either side approximately eighteen inches wide where the many cart wheels ran, and a raised, grass-covered ridge running the whole way down the centre. At the bottom, where the Crooked Road met the main road there was the traditional grass-covered triangle, formed by the carts moving either to the left up the Chapel Brae, or to the right towards the Post Office. This was fairly large and was a pleasant place to sit as children during the warm summer days.

I remember one occasion when I was very young standing at the top of the Chapel Brae, which was only a few yards from our door, watching in wonder a local man, called Long John after his great size, sitting there singing his head off. He was obviously on his way home from the local hostelry. As he sang he would lie back and kick his long legs up into the air. Eventually our next-door neighbour had to catch the horse and tackle it to the cart and go down and get him into it and take him up to the top of the Crooked Road where he lived.

I still remember clearly the sense of local astonishment the day a squad of men arrived, together with lorries, a tar-spreader, and a large steamroller to surface The Crooked Road. This astonishment was felt most by the older people who throughout all their long years had never known the Crooked Road as anything other than a grass-covered cart track, and who had never imagined that they would see the day when it would be surfaced like a main road. There was a general sense of "What is the world coming to!"

All byroads have, of course, long since been tarmacked and many of them carry as much traffic now as the main roads did then.

Ironically, it was the advent of tarmacadam that was eventually to spell the death-knell for Lislea Quarry. After it was introduced and had proved itself feasible more and more Local Authorities began to use it. The orders for road stone and setts from the quarry started to dwindle and eventually dried up completely.

Lislea Quarry was closed in 1929, some thirty years after it had first opened. All the machinery, including the stone-crushing plant, was removed and transported to Germany. All that was left was the stone-built receptacle of the granulator, at the top of which all the various grades of stone had been stored. The iron sluices beneath each section, under which the carts and lorries used stop to be loaded up, have long since rusted into a solid mass.

In 1979, the year of the centenary of Lislea Church, Lislea Dramatic Society decided to put on a stage show as part of the celebrations. One half of this was devoted to some of the more significant events that had affected the lives of the people in the hundred years since the Church was built. It was decided to include Lislea Quarry in this. I had already written the outline of a poem that would be part of the stage presentation. I needed to get photographs from the quarry that I would mount as slides and project on stage, and also stones to simulate the quarrying and the sett-cutting. I went down to the quarry one evening and walked its full length. I was surprised to find that there were still stones and pieces of rock lying loose along some sections of the floor. The rest was almost completely overgrown with grass, weeds, and gorse, as is the whole floor now. I hadn't walked far until I came across pieces of rock with the clear, vertical imprints of the chisels with which they had been split, and also pieces of flat stone with neat chisel-holes bored through their centre. I also found a number of setts, some unfinished, along the bank of the river where the sett-cutters used work.

As I looked at these stones, especially those that bore the chisel imprints, it was almost impossible not to think of the hands that had fashioned them, hands of men then long since gone. It struck me that in the case of many of them this may have been the only evidence that they left behind of their existence, their signatures carved on now forgotten stones.

As I looked along the expanse of the granite face, stretching some four hundred yards, I began to see in my mind the groups of men strung out along it working; some prising the rock from above with hammers, chisels and wedges; others breaking it down into small roughly shaped sections; others hauling these to the groups of cutters who inexorably chiselled away fashioning the setts; others breaking down the remainder into road stone with large sledgehammers, to be replaced later by the rock crusher and the conveyor belt. It was as if the quarry had come alive again for a memorable few minutes, and I found the scene to be a slightly disturbing one. I was watching men who had pitted themselves against this hard, and virtually unyielding, granite face, nine hours per day, six days per week, over a period of some thirty years; a life that struck me then as being closer to a mere form of existence than to living. As I was finishing and about to leave a flock of birds swept overhead, from west to east across the quarry face, their song accentuated in the vacant silence of the growing twilight. Somehow it seemed a fitting close.

I jotted down those images as they occurred and they came to form the central core of the piece below. This was dramatised on stage in the autumn of 1979 with the accompaniment of slides, songs, a large backdrop of the quarry, and groups of local men, all tradesmen, who kept a rhythmic background beat of chisel striking stone in time with the words.

THE QUARRY

There is no wisdom in these stones,
Nothing to be gleaned
Of truth or pity
Or the indomitable spirit
Save the pain of those
Who beat upon the rock
Forcing it to fall back
A yard or two
From their decades" assault,
The rubble of retreat

Their sole victory, cold
Comfort for the rout of bones
And broken lives.
Each generation sending
Reinforcements to the front
Flinging in the youth
To season on the rock's
Hard edge.

Today, on a quiet evening
When the harsh contours are honed
On the sinking sun
The dark face turns
A deceptive smile
To the present descendants
Of those ground men,
Possessing a strange beauty of its own,
Almost winning forgiveness,
And when the stillness
Spreads soft fingers
Along Slieve Gullion's ridges
You can almost hear the distant echoes
Drift through quiet years
Until the incubating silence
Hatches them into being,
The distant ring of steel on stone
the squat groups of anchored men
Hammering out their setts,
And quarrying ages of forgiveness.

To this rock they came
These hard-faced men of fruitless vision
To barter life for existence,
Muscle chiselled on the wind,
Bones as sharp as flint,
Clinging to the indomitable rock.

Here in this corner
Beartlai Dearg and O' Brien
Old Pat Hannaway and Magennis
Gnawed their setts in unison,
Turning chisel to the hammer blow,
Playing out
Their rhythmic symphony of hope,
And further up the granite face
The stone was chewed and pulped
Into a refined dust
To spread on distant roads
Their feet would never go,
Slewed along on conveyor belt
To the receptacle above,
Its bulk weighing heavy
On the minds of those
Who carted it the seven blood miles
To Newry town
For two shillings per load.

The hands that drilled these holes
Are silent now,
The elongated toothmarks in the rock
Where chisel bit on stone
The tongueless Ogham of their lives
Uttering silent whispers
Along the silent rows
With only the birds to break
Their eternal reverie
Flinging notes of hope
Against the silent wall.

But still their setts survive,
The indomitable trademark of their skill.
Far off in Newry town
They group and muster

Holding out a stubborn frontier
Along the Mall, aged,
Long-forgotten sentinels of time.
And still in Belfast city
In a sophisticated setting
Along loud shelves of learning
A chunk of basalt rock
Proclaims its origin,
"Early Neolithic,
Result of lava cooling,
Quarried at Lislea".

Acknowledgement: *I wish to acknowledge my indebtedness to the booklet "Lislea Church and Community", edited by T.B. Keane, for names and dates relating to Lislea Quarry in the above article.*

Time and Place

The past is a strange place. We stumble on it with surprise in childhood and never quite manage to accommodate ourselves fully to it. It always retains the power to surprise and enchant. I think that many of us deep down, if we are to be honest, have a kind of subconscious feeling that life only began when we were born, or at least only properly got started. Events before that time can often seem unreal. They lie in a kind of myopic, mystical world. In my own case, I remember having the distinct feeling that nothing of much significance could have happened before 1940. How could it when I wasn't there?

How many of us, for example, can imagine our parents as young children going to school, or even stranger, as new-born infants held in mothers' arms? Parents come ready-made, as we first know them. That, I think, is why old photographs are so fascinating, especially when they deal with people whom we already know. They give us a brief, but shafting glimpse, into this other world, a world that is closer to the world of imagination than to that of reality.

Some years ago I came across a photograph of my father when he was in his early thirties. He was a complete stranger to me, sitting up straight and sophisticated in a photographer's studio, dressed from head to toe in exquisitely matching striped grey suit, waistcoat, stockings, gleaming shoes, stiff white collar, dickey bow, and gold watch chain. This was a man whom I had never seen throughout my life, except perhaps on Sunday, wearing anything other than rough working clothes, mud stained boots, and battered hat as he toiled away virtually non-stop along the frontier of existence. I never saw any evidence that he had any sense of dress or indeed any time for such meaningless nonsense. But here he was staring out at me, a complete, carefree dandy, with the world still at his feet.

The sense of mysticism associated with the past is the reason, I think, why I was enchanted from my earliest childhood by stories, not stories from books, but real stories, told by real people, the kind that I heard virtually every night in our house, which was a céilí house. All stories by their very nature deal with the past and when you are a child this means with that unseen, vaguely imagined world before your time.

Someone in the céilí house would start off a tale with words such as "I remember, thirty years ago", — and then look around for a time peg on which to hang it– "when I was about the age of that lad there", pointing either to my brother or myself, and then continue with his story. Anyone who could say, "I remember, thirty years ago —" had my immediate attention. I would look at him with a sense both of wonder and of awe. How could anyone be talking about things that happened thirty years ago when you are only seven?

I would be carried back on the wings of the story into this distant and scarcely believable world and it would be brought to life before me. This was not a made-up, or mythical, event. This man saw it. He was there. He was part of it!

It would inevitably come the turn of an older member in the céilí house to tell a tale. He would raise the ante even further and start off with words that were scarcely credible, "I remember, fifty years ago, when I was in my teens —" Fifty years ago. That was an eternity, beyond any form of calculation! It must put him somewhere in the time range of Finn Mc Cool!

This inability of young children to differentiate between different levels of the past was brought home to me many years later when my own son came home from school, when he was around five years of age, and asked, "Daddy, did you know John the Baptist?" As it turned out I didn't, but I could see clearly the logic of his thinking. John the Baptist was ancient, so he knew straight away someone who must have first hand knowledge of him, his father, for he was thirty-five.

It comes now almost with a shock of incredulity to realise that if the céilí house were still going I could join the elders and raise the ante even further. There are many stories that I could start off with the words, "I remember, sixty years ago —", and still have a number of years to spare.

I remember sixty years ago watching the American soldiers marching down our road, four abreast, two or three times per week, each of them carrying an enormous pack on his back, and four of them walking in a straight line supporting a long pole on one shoulder. It never struck me to wonder what the long pole was for. American soldiers always carried a long pole. Even in later adulthood I was never quite sure exactly what it was for, the central support for a large tent, perhaps, which they pitched at night, which would explain part, at least, of the large packs.

They invariably stopped at our house, took off their backpacks and sat down on the step outside the front door and along the low walls, with me sitting in the middle of them. I was always attracted by their strange accents and friendly attitude, but more by the sweets and chocolate which they always seemed to carry with them.

My mother would boil water for them to make their tea. That was the first time I saw the small double-sided tins, with a lid on either end, one side for sugar, the other side for tea, which were to become common for a period during and after the war.

I remember as clearly, literally, as yesterday the day the war ended; a car, probably the only one in the area, driving up and down the road with men standing on the runner-board on either side shouting the news that the war was over.

The years of storytelling in the céilí house opened up the past to me in a vivid way, just as one might open a large door into a strange and enchanting place. As it turned out I was destined to spend a good deal of my later life either writing or speaking about this very subject, and particularly about the great legends and heroic figures which were moulded from the landscape of South Armagh, and how the influences working in them could still be seen in the people of my youth. I would count the céilí house as the largest single influence on my life. It was the receptacle of the true history of my people, the only place in reality where that history could have been recorded, in the oral tradition.

Normal history does not deal with this. To be fair it does not have the scope to do so. It must focus its attention on major events and significant figures, dates, economic trends, wars, land acquisitions, the refashioning of the world through many different generations.

It does not have time to get down to the grass roots of history, to the ordinary people, their trials, tribulations, traditions, inherited values, aspirations, and changing outlook. Many would argue that it is here that true history lies, for, ironically, it is these very people who in the end analysis often have the largest single influence on the course of history. It is they who have to bear it and its consequences and it is they who slowly, and almost imperceptibly, finally change it. This is becoming ever more apparent as time goes on, and especially when politicians have learned the bitter lesson that if they lose touch with the ordinary man, great historical edifices which they are in the process of building can come crumbling down around them.

One thing I regret very much, as in the case of the gypsies on the Crooked Road, about whom I speak in a different section, is that I was not older at the time of the céilí house, so that I might have recorded the stories told by these men and have pushed the narrators further and deeper into the storehouse of their memories. However, even then I would still be losing out for there is no proper time to start recording oral history. No matter when you start it will be too late. The optimum time is always now.

I have spent forty years of my life teaching, nearly all of them in Grammar Schools. On many occasions throughout that time, when I suddenly got fed up toiling away at the normal grind, I would tell the pupils, on the spur of the moment, to close their books and say to them something like, "How many of you have ever heard the story of the witch, the Cailleach Beara, on the top of Slieve Gullion?" There would be instantaneous silence.

I would start and tell them about Culann and his two daughters and how both of them were in love with Finn Mc Cool, and how one of them played a spiteful trick on the other by casting a spell on the waters of the lake on the top of Slieve Gullion while Finn was in retrieving a ring that she said had fallen from her finger so that when he put his foot on dry land he was turned into a withered old man. The story would continue to tell of how Finn got back his strength and original form, in everything except his hair. This would lead into stories of Culann himself and of the High King for whom he worked, Conor Mac Neasa, which in turn would lead to Cuchulainn and the Red Branch Knights etc. etc.

Throughout the narration of these stories there would be complete and utter silence in the class. People who before that might have been fidgeting or whispering to their neighbour would be completely absorbed in the unfolding events. When the bell would ring to mark the end of the period there would be a reaction which you would never hear at any other time, a spontaneous groan going up from the whole class.

This used to fascinate me. How, in a modern and fairly cynical society, could stories of such a simple and almost mythical nature have such an immediate impact on the minds of students? In addition to that, not wishing to cast aspersions on any other schools, the Grammar School intake, was held to represent the top five to ten per cent of the intellectual ability of each generation. These were pupils, therefore, who represented a cross section of the future leaders of society. You would expect them to consider such stories to be beneath their intelligence, almost like fairy tales. This did not prove to be the case. In fact, I often told them fairy tales, or at least stories about the fairies, their origins, their influences on the minds of the people of Ireland, and the superstitions surrounding them to this day, many of which they themselves were already aware of. They also found these fascinating. So, what is it then about the past that has such a fascination for the human mind? I am not quite sure. It is as if we have a latent affinity with antiquity, perhaps with our own ancestry, registered somewhere in our genes. The more mystical and otherworldly the stories, such as ghost stories, the greater they seem to attract.

I found the above reaction to stories told in class to be the same over a wide area. I found it not only in the Abbey School in Newry, where I spent most of my years teaching, but also in Ballinahinch, Dungannon, Armagh, and Dundalk. I found it also in every year group, from first year right up to A Level.

In fact each year when I received a new A level class, many of whom I may not have taught myself, I always made a point of spending the whole of the first week giving them a kaleidoscopic view of Ireland's linguistic, cultural, and social history, which in this country were inextricably linked. In this I would start with the movement of the Celts across Europe, their arrival in Ireland, their contact with the Tuatha De Danann, the rise of the great Celtic

Legends, the major pagan worship, the Bardic Schools, the full-time professional scholars, the great cultural, linguistic and land changes of the 17th century, the introduction of the freer Amhrán poetic meter, the last great poets of the Gaelic Era in the 18th century, together with celebrated writers of the new era, modern day literature.

In a long story, of which the above are only a few scratched headings, I found the interest of the pupils over the period to be abiding. Parts of the story they found completely fascinating, mostly, I think, because prior to this they did not know that they had a history. When the story would be finished you normally ended up with a class of pupils who were aware that the language which they were about to start studying at a higher level was something more than a mere collection of words and grammatical rules, but rather a receptacle of the past, of history, of identity, and of themselves.

I have said often to students that, irrespective of whether they are aware of it or not, or irrespective of whether they even believe it or not, it is a very clear and irrefutable fact that they are the end-product of all that has gone before them. If a link in the chain had been broken anywhere along the line, even two thousand years ago, they would not be here now. Ancestry has travelled a very long, and often very arduous, journey to get them to where they now are. I think it is completely unrealistic to assume that, if young people do not know something about where they have come from, they are in a position to make an informed and balanced judgement as to where they should be going.

The past of our own lives also holds a fascination for us all, especially as we get older. This is seen clearly when groups of people meet, especially those who haven't seen each other for a number of years. They may make a fleeting reference to the present, none whatsoever to the future, and delve straight away into the past, as they recall event after event from their early years. The farther back the stories go the better. Often many of them can hardly wait until the others finish so that they can start telling their own reminiscences. It is as if they are reliving their lives in these stories, almost as if they see themselves now as different people, and hours can pass like minutes. This fixation with the past in our own lives is more, I think, than mere nostalgia. We seem to be much more at ease with the past than any other time. The reason is that we have met the past and got to know it, and, irrespective of the number of bleak periods it may have held, we have managed somehow or other to get through it. By contrast, the future always remains a stranger and we never quite know how to prepare adequately for its coming. As for the present, it is simply the point which the past has reached up to now.

Some years ago I went through a fairly seminal experience. I was teaching at the time in the Abbey Grammar School in Newry. The Ministry of Education had changed the rules concerning what students could study in English as part of their G.C.S.E. curriculum. In poetry teachers were given the option of doing poetry of a local nature, instead of one of the compulsory poets. The English teacher, Mr. Pat Mooney, decided to make a selection of poetry suitable for that age group from an anthology of mine, "Where Ditches Meet", which he himself had edited. He put together a book entitled "The Broken Wall", with a special introduction and background explanatory notes, illustrated by pupils from the Art Department. This book was studied in the Abbey and a number of adjoining schools.

When he had the poems completed in class Mr Mooney came to me one day and told me that he would like to take the students out to the Ring of Gullion where the poems were composed and asked me if I would accompany them and act as a guide. Although I agreed readily I had deep reservations about it.

I had been teaching in the Abbey for many years and no one would have known that I had written anything until then. In addition, I had a number of the pupils concerned in my own Irish group. They were not people whom I would consider to be in any way sentimental, or poetically minded, to say the least. They were honest, down-to-earth, "hard men". I felt that I was in for a hiding-to-nothing here, and that most of the day would be spent listening to much sniggering and behind-the-hand whispering, or worse.

When the day finally arrived I led the group to places where I could point out various aspects of the terrain which had influenced the poems. In a number of cases I was able to bring them to the actual spot where a particular poem was conceived. Such a one was the piece entitled "A Hero Fallen". This was composed in Donnelly's top mountain field one day in spring when I sat down on the grass for a rest after inspecting cattle which I had there. The opening part of this poem goes as follows:-

I have sat among the flowers of May
Along whin-clad ditches
As the rabbits shyly nibbled
Among the broken ridges
Of a long-forgotten field.

And from the briared rivers
Came the sound of water,
Rhythmic larynx of the mountain
Keeping tune with Heaven,
And from a distant meadow
A corncrake plucked the silence
Strumming his sweet hoarseness
Along the quiet grass —

When the group reached the spot the mountain was on their right hand side, with the clear outline of ancient ditches visible. Along the foot of the mountain and across the bottom of the field, a few yards from where I had sat, were two mountain streams, with the running water clearly audible. Looking across this they were looking into the open valley with a variegated assortment of fields. I was able to point out to them the actual meadow from which the corncrake had called.

As they looked out from that spot what they were looking at was the poem itself, lying before them in the landscape, real and simple, devoid of any pretence or sophistication.

I then took them to a raised spot and pointed out a number of the houses which had appeared in the poems; Mickey's house, Kearney's, Mc Cann's, Pat O' Brien's, all lying in a neat circle around them.

We then took them in the bus to many other locations, along the Mountain Road to Calmor's Rock, and up Courtney Road behind Lislea Mountain and across to the Crooked Road. They were amazed to find that the Crooked Road, which figured in a number of poems actually existed and that that was its official name. We stopped at the top corner of the road where there was a clear view of the sweeping valley, right into the Gap of The North, and I filled them in on other poems that featured that terrain, and also told them a little of the legends associated with the area.

The last stop at the end of the evening was the shed in which I had composed the poem "Father". This was a shed which my father had planned often and spoken about but never lived to start. It was a renovation and extension of an old existing building. Shortly after his death my brother and myself carried out the job. As I stood one day sawing a piece of timber when the undertaking was nearing completion I began to imagine my father there. I could hear in my mind his voice as he surveyed the work, and for a brief few moments it was as if he were actually present. This reverie was rudely shattered when I paused to get my breath and looked up:-

> *I look up*
> *And the words freeze*
> *On the door's mouth*
> *As through the awning*
> *The gravestones tongue*
> *Their rejection.*

When the students had entered the shed Mr. Mooney told them to turn round and look out. The surprise was clearly visible on many faces when they found that they were looking straight at Lislea graveyard, and that the doorway was in direct line with my father's headstone.

The reaction of the whole group that day took me completely by surprise. Throughout all the time we spent travelling around there wasn't even a hint of a snigger, or a laugh, or background whisper. The reaction was as near as it could be to the very opposite of what I had imagined. From the outset there was an immediacy of interest, enthusiasm, enquiry and often surprise, as they identified different things which had appeared in the poems. Never before had I seen the "hard men" so engaged in any classroom in which I had met them. When we reached the end of the journey at the bottom of the Crooked Road there was a flurry of further questions about places we had been or things I had said.

As the group pulled away I was left, I have to admit, in a state of puzzled bewilderment. Why had I just witnessed what I had seen? It gave me cause to ponder for quite some time afterwards, and taught me also a salutary lesson.

I came to the realisation that for those students that was probably the first time that what goes under the heading of education, especially poetry, became real for them; the first occasion when time and place met as one.

Up until then poetry was something that, as far as they were concerned, existed only inside the pages of a book. In so far as they would even think of it having been written, they would imagine that its author would be someone distant and ethereal, someone writing about great events or, as Kavanagh would say, about important times and important places. For the first time in their lives they realised that poetry was what you see when you look out the window; that it was about basic things, about life, about what is, — an attempt to record something of the landscape of time, place, and people.

I realised that the vast majority of the education that we dish out in classrooms never comes close, or even remotely close, to the basic bedrock of reality, but remains in a form of disembodied abstraction.

For the first time I also realised how fortunate I was to have spent so many years of my life teaching a subject where the occasional indulgence in the fantasy of fairytale romance, legendary figures, heroic deeds, and mystical events was always relevant, either directly in the case of A Level students, or indirectly in the case of the rest. This relevance was woven through the fabric of the language and through the background of the students themselves.

Many of these legends represent the earliest form of recorded history in Ireland, which was recorded inside the vernacular tradition only for many centuries before the advent of the written word. Although many of the original historical events were gradually consumed by the growing legends a central core of them still remains. For example, it is here that we learn many detailed events concerning the first century King of Ulster, and later High King of Ireland, Conor Mac Neasa. There are sufficient facts still remaining to show clearly the type of character he was, how he worked his way by deceit to the position of King of Ulster, and how many important people he offended throughout the whole of Ireland by his Machiavellian attitude, duplicity, and numerous broken promises on his way to the position of High King. That would explain why there were so many tribal leaders from all over the south of Ireland so willing to throw their support behind Meave and Ailill in their attack on Ulster, and consequently Conor, under the guise of the so-called quest for the Bull of Cooley. Whatever about the bull, I have no doubt that there is a central core of historical fact running through those legends.

These historical tales could only have been preserved inside the protective security of the oral tradition, a tradition whose vibrancy for a period of some two thousand years guaranteed their preservation. They still have the edge over their compatriot, formal history, in their ability to stimulate and captivate. I have absolutely no doubt whatsoever that if I were to choose any one of the groups of students I have mentioned above and go into their classroom and start reading the formal history of the North, including that of South Armagh, they would be yawning with boredom after five minutes. For some reason that never happens with oral history. It seems to have managed down through the centuries to preserve both its mystique and its allure.

In the past I have had occasion to lead many groups of people through the Ring of Gullion. This started in the early seventies during one of the celebrations being held for the Gaelic poets of the 18th century. With the passage of time these groups became much larger and much more frequent. The participants came from a very wide area. I suppose there was scarcely a county in Ireland that wasn't represented somewhere along the line, together with a considerable number of groups from America.

The initial response of these groups, especially those from abroad, caused me some small embarrassment. Their spontaneous and effusive reaction, not only to the many stories associated with the area, but also to the outstanding beauty of the whole landscape made me realise that I had long since become so used to it that I was taking it for granted. I was forced to see my own area again through their eyes, the eyes of people who were seeing it for the first time, and to realise that it was, indeed, a remarkable landscape in many ways.

The terrain of the Ring of Gullion was originally formed more than sixty million years ago by a period of sustained volcanic eruptions, thought to have lasted upwards of three million years. These produced a large volcanic cone eight miles in diameter. During the last ice age when the dense sheets of ice which covered the whole area, as they did the majority of the North, began to move, two large glaciers ploughed their way south eastwards through the cone leaving the large mass of immovable basalt rock, known as Slieve Gullion, behind. This left a landscape dominated at its centre by this mountain, with a ring of smaller hills and mountains surrounding it on all sides. These were once part of the outer crust of the original volcanic cone, now known as the Ring Dyke.

This landscape still bears the scars of its ancient origin, a multifarious collection of hills, valleys, scoured rocks, and mountain passes through which a lot of the history of Ireland once passed. It is no wonder that when the Celts arrived in Ireland they should have chosen this spot to locate some of their greatest legends. The landscape was as mystical as the stories which they wove around it. It was destined to produce larger-than-life figures not only in our early history but down into modern times.

We always started our trip at Calmor's Rock at the northern end of the Ring, and finished in Creggan graveyard in the south. After telling the tale of the notorious highwayman, Cathal Mór, whose main hideout was at this rock, a story which I have already recounted in another place, I would take the group down to my own house where we would park the bus in the yard and walk up the fields behind to the hill above. At this point you were surrounded by mountains on all sides with the full sweep of the western valley laid out before you, right into the Gap of the North. It was an excellent place for storytelling as you could point directly to many landmarks associated with different legends.

There before us was Slieve Gullion, the mountain on which the young lad Séadanda had killed the massive hound of Culann and as a consequence received his later renowned name Cuchulainn, the Hound of Culann; on the top of the mountain the lake where Culann's daughter turned the young Finn Mc Cool into a wizened old man; just over the brow of the mountain to the left the place where Saint Moninna built what is considered to be the first Church in Ireland, a fact that gave its name to the town land where it was situated, Cill Shléibhe, modern day Killeavy; to the right where the tail of the mountain sweeps down to Faughart the place where the most celebrated female Saint in Ireland was born and reared, Saint Brigid; on the face of the same mountain a number of places where Saint Oliver Plunkett said mass during the years when he was forced to go on the run between 1674 and 1679, and also the south cairn on the top of the mountain which was one of his main hideouts during that time. From this spot alone we are looking, inside a fairly short space, at the terrain of three Saints, something, I suppose, which is fairly unusual in itself.

With a sweep to the right we are looking up through the Gap of the North. Across this ran the earliest man-made fortification in Ireland, The Black Pig's Dyke. This earthen rampart, which predated Cuchulainn by approximately a hundred years, once connected all the natural barriers of mountains, lakes, marshes etc. to create a continuous line of protection from Dundalk to Roscommon, cutting off the men of the North, the Fir Uladh, from all the men of the South, the Fir Éireann. Beyond that barrier line stood Cuchulainn as he held off the forces of Meave and Ailill.

Through the same gap Hugh O' Neill would later lead the forces of O' Neill and O' Donnell against Essex in the celebrated rising of the Earls in 1595, finally leading to their destruction at Kinsale in 1601. In 1641 the gap was again seized by the O' Neills in the second rising. This gave them control over the land passage into Ulster which allowed them a large degree of success until the arrival of Cromwell. In 1690 it was down through this same pass that Marshal Schomberg led the forces of William of Orange on his way to the battle of the Boyne, where a century of Ireland's history was finally settled.

If you draw back a little from there down the valley, you have a clear view of the location of some of the great poets of the 18th century who were left to record in their poems and songs the passing of the Gaelic era. On the left in Forkhill was Peadar Ó Doirnín; in the centre around Mullabawn was Pádraig Mac A' Liondáin; to the right in Creggan was the best loved poet of them all, Art McCooey; and a short distance over the mountain to the left was the blind poet Séamas Dall Mac Cuarta.

As we draw back farther down the valley we see the house in which the famous Bishop of Dromore, Patrick Donnelly, better known as the Bard of Armagh, spent twenty two years of his life in disguise under constant pain of death after his appointment as Bishop in 1697 until his death in 1719.

This is also the house in which the last native Gaelic speaker in the area, Sally Humphries, spent her married life, dying in 1918.

Along these same hills roamed some of the most famous Raparees of the 17th century, especially the legendary Séamas Mór Mc Murphy and Count Redmond O' Hanlon, and the not so famous blagards, such as Cathal Mór.

A landscape of extremes, both physically and culturally, the Ring of Gullion seems to have something in it for everyone. Its stories never cease to fascinate, especially strangers who have never visited the area before. As we stood often on the hill behind our house moving around in a circle through time and history the stories would be coming thick and fast, with pieces of poetry thrown in perhaps as well, depending on the mood, to complement the tales.

I remember on one occasion, as we made our way back down the fields towards the bus, an American lady catching up with me and saying, almost in a whisper, "I never thought I would ever hear poetry recited live out in a field". I was about to make some flippant rejoinder, as would be my wont, until I saw her face and realised how serious she was. It struck me straight away that, whereas for us it was very natural to hear poetry out in a field, something we had done on so many occasions, for her it was quite a different matter. This lady was from New York, a city of skyscrapers. There was a good chance that she may never have stood in a field before, not to mention hearing poetry recited in it. There was something about the word "live" that got me. It gave me a brief but incisive image of crowded places, and stuffy rooms, and a lifestyle completely different to our own. I had a feeling almost of sadness that something so small, and to me so trivial, should have meant so much to her, and also a great sense of satisfaction that I had chosen to recite some poetry on that occasion. During a later trip I found that the tables were turned on me in this regard.

On that occasion I was taking a group of students from a university in the South of Ireland on the usual tour. The trip had almost come to an end as we stood in Creggan graveyard around the tombstone of Art McCooey. Of all the famous people buried in Creggan the graveyard is most closely associated with McCooey. It was here that he wrote his best-known and celebrated poem ÚrChill An Chreagáin, on one of the occasions that he was forced to hide out from Johnston of the Fews. Although the poem is an Aisling, or Vision Poem, in Art's case it is closer to a poem of escapism. In it he puts into the mouth of the Heavenly Maiden all his own hopes and aspirations. In what was a life of turbulence and penury, ending at the tragic age of 36, there is only one of those aspirations that we can be sure for certain was ever fulfilled, the one expressed in the last two lines of his poem:

> "Má éagaim fán tSeanainn, i gcrích Mhanainn nó san Éiphte mhór
> Gurb i gcill chumhra an Chreagáin a leagfar mé i gcré faoi fhód."
> Should I die 'round the Shannon, in Manannan, or on Egypt's wide shore,
> 'Midst the fair Gaels of Creggan may I rest in true peace for evermore.

When I had finished recounting the facts of Art's life, finishing with the above lines someone in the crowd struck up the first bars of ÚrChill An Chreagáin. The rest all joined in and they sang it the whole way through, standing around Art's grave.

This poem/song is a personal favourite of mine and I have heard it sung on numerous occasions, mostly by professional singers on elaborate stages, but I have never heard it sung as it was that day by a group of ordinary people standing on a grass-covered bank in the ancient graveyard of Creggan. It had a sense of immediacy and poignancy that could not be created on any stage. The song had come home, back to its grass roots, to the place where it was conceived, sung at the feet of its composer, a coincidental but striking meeting point of time and place.

The Ring of Gullion is a landscape where time often seems to stand still. It is as if the landscape has managed to record in its myriad hills, mountains, dells and valleys the history to which it had stood witness from its ancient birth, a polyglot of figures in which our identity is enshrined; legendary heroes, pagan Gods, Christian Saints, brigands, scholars, highwaymen, poets, and major historical figures who, for good or ill, shaped the destiny not only of this area but of Ireland as a whole.

As I stood on the hill with many different groups, with the tales of these figures sweeping around our ears, they seemed as alive as they were almost two thousand years ago. If one of them were suddenly to be seen walking across the summit of Slieve Gullion he would not seem entirely out of place. If we were to plot our own lives against the graph of this terrain's sixty million years, our beginning and our end would fall so closely together that it would not be possible to represent them. The smallest dot, even an invisible one, would be too large. In this landscape which in a thousand years from now will be much the same as it is today, just as it was a thousand years ago, the past, present, and future seem to roll together into one, here where time and place stand forever with arms entwined in an eternal embrace.

PRESENCES

No lens snapped them as they tramped
And churned their print in the thundering
Ground, lances flashing to the
Wild roar of "treise lámh" or some
Would-be-wrong righted

Or supremacy benighted beneath the
Flaying flash, but their presences
Were stamped. The processing room
Of darkened fields and low-set hills
Of a lurking autumn twilight

Processes their negative, the
Thundering clouds their roar. The eye that sees
Welcomes their horror and splendor,
Caresses the pain and ignorance
And honour of their blighted glory.

Slieve Gullion still bears the hoary
Beauty of Culann's daughters and the
Wild fancy that sent Finn flying
Into the murky waters for the honour
Of a hero's geasa. The intimacy

Blunted now by the refined ignorance
Of eyes gazing from tourist parks
And the castrated contours of imposed
Order. But the peaks still thunder, their
Clenched fist raised in triumph or warning.

They are the breed of Balor, fierce, heartless,
Freezing time in a formorian stare.
Threatening those who dare
To forget their pride, their strength,
Their fierce nobility.

The Gypsies

During my childhood in the 1940's gypsies were such a commonplace in South Armagh that they were almost a permanent fixture in the social landscape. These were the "real gypsies", the original travelling people, long before the advent of caravans, to be followed later by lorries, trucks and industrial machinery. These people carried all their possessions with them piled on a single cart, pulled by horse or pony, and lived by the traditional arts of begging and tinsmith work.

These true nomadic people had an ancestry stretching back at least to the 17th century, to the period of plantations and evictions when many families had no option but to take to the roads for survival. Since, however, a common name amongst them was Ward, from the Irish "Mac A' Bhaird" – "Son of the Bard", there is a suggestion that some of them, at least, may have stretched back much farther in history, to a distinguished and noble ancestry.

The traditional camping ground for the gypsies in our area was along the Crooked Road. The various groups seemed to follow an annual cycle, always appearing in rotation through different times of the year. There would be relatively few periods without some group or other making a path to our door. It would happen occasionally that two, or more, groups would arrive at the same time, something that would put a major strain on local generosity.

Begging was a supreme art and was done exclusively by the women. They always wore long flowing dresses with a heavy plaid shawl wrapped around their heads and shoulders. Couched in the shawl there would nearly always be a small infant, and by the mother's side a young child five or six years old, the mandatory prerequisites of the begging trade. They were always barefoot, even in the coldest or wettest weather.

Even as a child I used marvel at the women's skill in begging, especially their dauntless persistence. Their requests at the door would always be accompanied by promises of many prayers that would be said for the potential benefactor, and frequent references to either the infant in the shawl or the child by their side — "A wee drop of milk for the infant, missus, and may God look down on you and take care of you." When they would get the milk they would move to the next request— "Would you have some bread for the wee fellow here and I'll pray for you and for your own children that God may look after them and never see them come to any harm?" If this request were acceded to they would continue to the third one, with the prayer growing longer each time. "A few spuds for meself and himself and the childer, and may God and the Blessed Virgin watch over you and yours, and may you never suffer from illness or from hunger or from any evil in the world". They would keep persisting, irrespective of how many requests were granted, or how many protests were made by the giver, until the benefactor's patience eventually ran out. Even while the door was being closed they would still be persisting.

The gypsies were a completely different breed to us, living a lifestyle that we could scarcely imagine, and one that I know none of us could ever have endured. How the children, especially, survived tramping the roads barefoot, with only meagre clothing, through the bitterest of weather was a mystery. I remember one occasion, on a freezing cold day, when my mother's sympathy got the better of her. As the gypsy woman went around to the shed in the yard with my father to get potatoes, my mother took the wee lad, who was standing dripping wet on the doorstep in the biting cold, inside and put him standing beside the fire to warm him and dry out his clothes. When the mother returned she stormed into the house, something a gypsy would never do, with her eyes flashing with anger. "What are you doing!" she screamed at my mother, as she grabbed the child and pulled him back from the fire. My mother, greatly taken aback, replied that she was just letting him warm himself. "Do you want to kill my child?" She shouted. "Don't you know that this is not natural for him? Are you wanting him to catch pneumonia!" And she hastened out of the house in a fury.

The men folk were skilled tinsmiths. They would go from house to house selling instruments they had made, mostly cans of all sizes, pots, tins, tea drawers etc. They also did repair work. Any tin instruments where the bottoms had become worn and had started to leak were put aside to await the arrival of the next group of tinkers.

They always did the work on the spot, sitting on the step outside the door. I was always fascinated as a child watching them work, as they removed the old base carefully so as to leave the narrow flange at the bottom of the can in tact, and then unrolled a strip of tin and placed the can on top of it to trace out a new base.

They worked with the minimum of tools, mostly a tin cutter, a small hammer, and a round iron "knoll". They held the latter inside the can following the hammer as they tapped the edge of the new base up and over the bottom flange of the can. The edge and the flange were then beaten together tightly the whole way around the bottom rim of the can. No adhesive substance of any kind was ever used. When the job was finished the can would always be completely watertight and would remain so until the bottom itself wore out.

Being only eight or nine years old at the time I felt a certain apprehension when I had to pass the gypsies. Since a good deal of our land was adjacent to the Crooked Road this happened quite often, as one of my jobs was to bring the cows home in the evening. The tents were always pitched on the right hand side of the road with the carts heeled up behind them. In front of each tent there would be a fire, surmounted by a tripod with a kettle, or pot, hanging from a crook. The tripod was made of three thick sticks tied together at the top. Groups of people would be seated around each fire, on large stones or bits of log, engaged in animated discussion, accompanied by frequent laughter. On a Saturday night, when, I suppose, some refreshments were available, there would be much singing. Passers-by always went virtually unnoticed, unless they addressed the gypsies first.

I have only got a few regrets in my life. One of them is that I wasn't about fifteen years older when the era of the gypsies was at its height. What I wouldn't give now to be able to sit at one of those campfires and listen to their stories. What insight, I wonder, would they give into their closed, and almost secret, world? Would they have opened the door, even a little, on the mystery of their lives, on their tribal memories, on the inherited values that dictated their lifestyle? What view did they have of the world, from a life that was lived as close to nature as man could ever hope to get? What were their fears, their hopes, their aspirations? What qualities were prized most highly amongst them that set individuals apart? And most important of all, perhaps, what was their view of us, the housebound dwellers?

The only problems caused by the gypsies were to the farmers, and they always involved the ditches. At that time there was no such thing as fencing posts with barbed wire or sheep wire like today. All ditches had to be secured by "brearding". This was a very laborious and time-consuming task. It involved cutting bushes, hawthorn if possible, from the nearest point at which they were available and dragging them to the ditches. The top row of stones was removed from each ditch and the bushes were placed horizontally along the top, the butt of each bush being overlapped by the top of the next one. The stones were replaced on top of the bushes to secure them as the brearding continued. The gaps into the fields were also secured by bushes, normally one single large bush per gap, which could be rolled to one side to let the animals in or out and then pulled tight again by the butt, which was always left pointing towards the roadway. This was a job that was ongoing throughout the year as damaged bushes were renewed. In springtime, however, it was a very major task as all the ditches had to be rebrearded after the ravages of winter.

Once the gypsies arrived the trouble soon started. Although they could easily enough have procured their own firewood, the temptation of the ready-made, well-dried material close at hand was always too great. It wouldn't be long, despite repeated warnings from the farmers, until holes started to appear in the ditch fencing.

I remember one particular year, when I was around eight years old, it happened by chance that a number of groups of gypsies arrived in Lislea at the same time. Their camps were strung out along all the available space on the Crooked Road. It wasn't long until the trouble began. Despite many visits by my father and others, the bushes began disappearing from the ditches. Eventually every ditch was stripped bare, including the gaps, leaving the fields completely open to the road. Finally the farmers had had enough. The police were called, for the first time ever, to move the gypsies on.

It was after dark on a Saturday night in autumn when the police arrived. A number of local people, including my father and us children, had gathered. It was very unusual at that time to see policemen out in the country. It was even more unusual to feel, for the first time ever, that they did not pose a threat to us, that they were actually on our side. Silhouetted against the firelight in their full uniforms and peaked caps, with their glinting brass buckles and shining gun holsters, they constituted an awesome presence. As they moved from camp to camp telling the gypsies to gather their possessions and move on, the air was filled with the crying of children, the angry voices of men, and the constant pleading of women –

"It wasn't us, sir! We're dacent folk. We didn't touch your ditches. It was some of those other ones up above. Let us be, Sir!"

All these pleadings fell on deaf ears. The reply was always the same, "Get your stuff together and move on!" Some of the women would ask, "But where can we move to? Surely you don't expect us to get the wee ones out of bed at this time of night? Some of them are sick. Look, sir! Let us stay at least until the morning!"

No one listened. We all knew that they were gypsies and that gypsies always told lies. They had no option but to move on. We watched as the carts headed off one by one into the darkness, the children sitting bleary eyed on top of the bundled clothes. Eventually they were all gone, nothing left but the row of abandoned campfires winking in the night.

That scene remained with me for many years and troubled my conscience greatly. In the early 1980's I was asked by the Lislea Junior Drama Group to write a sketch for them for the Scor competition. I wrote "The Long Road", in which I tried to capture the essence of my feelings on that particular night. The sketch was performed on a number of occasions by the Lislea group, including in the local Scor competition, which they won that year.

THE LONG ROAD

Time: 1950.

SETTING:

A tinkers' camp in a field at the corner of a country road.

A low ditch runs along the back of the stage with a gap in the centre through which the road behind is visible. On the right of the gap is a low wide-mouthed tent. A child of about seven or eight is lying on rags at the opening of the tent with an old shawl thrown over it. Old clothes, bags etc. are hanging on the ditch.

Left of centre, towards the front, is a fire with a tripod made of sticks standing over it. A pot is suspended from a crook over the fire. Stones for sitting on are scattered around.

At right front is a harness and other trappings.

It is late evening.

The light comes up low on Bridget Casey on her hunkers at the fire stirring the pot. She is clad in old tattered garments, with a shawl thrown around her shoulders. Her boots are a couple of sizes too big, tied unevenly with cord.

As she stirs the pot she looks frequently over her shoulder with obvious anxiety. The child is twisting and turning. Finally the child moans and lets out a cry. Bridget jumps up quickly and goes over to it.

Bridget: There – there, child. Hush – hush. (Fixing the clothes on him.) Daddy won't be long. He'll surely have something for you this time. You'll be better soon. (She feels the child's head.) God, he's like a furnace! The fever must be getting worse. (Running to the ditch and pulling off old rags.) What is keeping you, Tim Casey! And me telling you to hurry. (Coming back with the rags.) It's meself should have gone to the market. It's worn out he'll be after sitting up all night working at the cans — and then the long journey before him. (Fixing the clothes on the child.) There, there, child.

Daddy won't let us down. Lie asy now. He won't be long. He'll have food for you and mebby medicine for the fever. — God, the heat of his poor wee head!

(Mr Burns enters with strong angry step. A thick-set farmer with hat back on his head and angry face. He is carrying a stout stick. Bridget starts up when she hears his step.)

Bridget: Tim —! (Taken aback.) Oh, it's yourself, sir —

Burns: Are you still here, Bridget Casey! Didn't you get your orders. How many times have you to be told to get off my land!

Bridget: But, sir, the child's sick. He has a raging fever. Burning like a furnace, sir. We couldn't move him till we get something for him —

Burns: None of your oul excuses, Bridget Casey, and your lies!

Bridget: As God is my judge, Mr Burns, sir. (Blessing herself.) Shur, it's the solemn truth I'm telling you. He has been burning this three days, and his wee face twisting with the pain of it. It's the hunger is the cause of it, sir. The hunger and the trampin —

Burns: — Go on out of that, you lying thief. It's too much yous get. A bit of hard work would be more in your line, like dacent folk who have to earn a living. (Looking around.) Where is that man of yours? Hiding again, I suppose —

Bridget: He's gone to the market to try and sell some cans to get something for the wee fellow. We have been trampin all week with scarcely a bite in our stomachs, only nettle broth and wild daughin — and everyone showing us the road, and himself scarcely fit to walk with the tiredness and the worry —

Burns: Tiredness! What would make him tired? Away in a pub, I suppose. Drinking and squandering the money that yous scrounge from dacent folk with your sad stories and your shenanagins.

Bridget: God forgive you, Mr. Burns, sir. A drop of drink never crosses Tim Casey's lips. Up all night he was, hammering away at the fire by moonlight till the dawn broke making cans for the market to-day to try to get a few shillings to buy food and medicine for the child, and him wild with worry. – It's our only son, Mr. Burns. The only thing we have in this world. Without him it's a long road we would be trampin —

Burns: Well, the sooner yous get tramping it the better. I don't want this field destroyed again like last year (Pulling clothes off the ditch with the point of his stick.) with your rags and your vermin.

Bridget: We never destroyed your field, sir. It must have been some other tinkers — them ones above on the hill. We're paceable folk. We wouldn't harm nothing.

Burns: Go on, Bridget Casey. You're all the same. I know yous well. You have been a scourge on me this years. Come on, get moving! (Pulling more clothes down.)

Bridget: (Running to pick up the clothes)   Have pity on us, Mr. Burns. Let us stay here a wee while longer – till we get the wee fellow better. No one else will help us. (Picking up a tin from the fire.)   And mebby you could spare a wee sup of milk for the child, and I'll say a prayer for yourself and your children, and God and his holy mother will smile on you and reward you and see that no sickness ever falls —

Burns: Haven't you the nerve, Bridget Casey! Is it trying to beg of me now you are as well? You refuse to leave my land, and me blue in the face telling you. Three times to-day I have been with you. And now you're trying to make a bloody fool of me all together. Well, I'll have no more of your oul trickery and your lies. (Pulling the clothes off the ditch roughly and kicking the harness. The child starts to cry.) Let yourself and Tim Casey be out of here straight away — and take your squalling brat with you, or I'll get the law to shift you.

Bridget: (Fearfully) Shur, you wouldn't take the law on innocent folk that would do no harm to no one. We're doing no injury to your land. Shur, it's only a small patch we need, sir. Only a place to sit and rest our bones. Surely there's room for us to do that in this wide world —?

Burns: You can find room somewhere else! I don't mind yous sitting. Yous can sit till the moss grows over your bones for all I care – provided yous don't sit on my land. I have no room for yous here. Get moving at once, Bridget Casey. (Moving off) At once, do you hear! And don't ever settle here again.

Bridget: But the child, sir. For the love of god, sir, the child! It's mebby dying he is — my only child — Have pity on us, sir! (She turns away in despair and goes over slowly to the child and knees down beside it. The child starts to whimper.) Hush, a leanbh. Ná caoin, a stór. Lie still now, child of my heart. The pain will soon be passing. (To herself) 'Tis worse he's getting. The eyes are going back in his head. – Oh, God, Tim Casey, what's keeping you!

(Tim enters slowly through the gap, head bent and dejected. He is a small, thin man, ragged and weather beaten. Exhaustion is clearly visible on his face. He has a bunch of cans tied with a rope on his back. He walks to the fire and slumps down on a stone.)

Bridget: (Jumping up) Tim! Thank God you're back. I thought you were never coming. (Seeing the cans. Horror in her voice.) Did you – did you not sell the cans!

Tim: No.

Bridget: No! (Running towards him) None – Not one? (Grabbing the cans and counting quickly) – four, five. Five! You sold none at all!

Tim: None.

Bridget: (Almost in tears) And food? Did you get food?

Tim: How would I get food? — I couldn't sell the cans.

Bridget: (Almost frantic) Did you not try beggin? Could you not —

Tim: I tramped all day, woman. To Toal's, Mc Cann's, Murphy's — everyone who used to give us something. Got hunted from every door with a litany of accusations and abuses flung after me.

Bridget: Accusations? But, shur, we never did anything. We never did any harm to anyone.

Tim: Well, someone did. Other tinkers must have been along the way. Our name is mud. There is no help for us here, woman.

Bridget: And what about the medicine? Did you try the doctor?

Tim: I was with him for an hour —

Bridget: — And did he give you something?

Tim: No. I would have to pay.

Bridget: But, isn't the medicine free? I thought —

Tim: It is. But you need a certificate to get it.

Bridget: Certificate?

Tim: Some paper or other with a number on it that proves that you were born, or something. I don't know! When you don't have it you have to pay —

Bridget: How much? — How much?

Tim: Two pounds.

Bridget: Two pounds! Where in the name of God would we get two pounds! – Mebby — mebby if you told him how bad the child is — that, — that he might die without it?

Tim: I told him that, woman. I did everything but go on my knees to him. It was no good. He said it was regulations. Unless you have the certificate —

Bridget: But what's all this talk about a certificate? Shur, we were born, Tim —

Tim: Unless you have proof – unless you're registered to prove it, (With emphasis) he can't give the medicine without the two pounds.

Bridget: (Moving towards the child) Two pounds. Surely there's somewhere we can get two pounds. (On her knees stroking the child's head) Surely you are worth that, child.

Tim: (Rising) How is he now? Is the fever any better?

Bridget: It's worse he's getting, I'm thinking. I'm getting scared, Tim. There is a terror seizing me, — a dark foreboding running through my bones. What if he should – if he should die, Tim!

Tim: (Walking towards her quickly, fear in his voice) Don't be silly, woman! He won't die. (Pushing her to one side) — He can't die! (Putting his arm under the child and lifting him towards him) And he that was so strong a while ago, — stepping out on the road before us, — leading the horse like a man.

Bridget: But look at him now, Tim. Look at the thinness of him and the wee pale face. I'm afraid, Tim — I'm afraid!

Tim: (Voice rising) He'll be all right, I'm telling you! (Cradling the child to him) He'll walk the roads soon again, you'll see, — stepping out before me over the hills of the morning. All he needs is a bit of food in his stomach. (Looking up) What have you in the pot, woman?

Bridget: Nettle broth.

Tim: Nettle broth! Is there no food at all —

Bridget: How would there be food? Wasn't I depending on you to have it with you when you came? (Moving towards the pot) Mebby a drop of the broth —

Tim: It's no good, woman!

Bridget: Well, we must do something. There must be someone — Father Maguire!

Tim: What?

Bridget: Father Maguire! You remember – on the road behind? (Pulling her shawl around her) 'Twas he that baptised the wee fellow. He'll help. (Moving quickly)

Tim: Bridget! (She pauses and looks back) Hurry, woman! (Exit Bridget. Tim fixes the clothes around the child)

Hold on me wee man. We'll soon have you better. Shur, what would I do without me main helper? I'd have no one to lead out the horse at the crack of dawn, or to run for sticks in the evening when I'm pitching the tent, or to pester me ears about the wonders of the world around the fire at night. (Stroking the child's head) And no one to run the hills before me, filling my steps with your laughter. – (Looking around) A bit of food is all you need. (He goes over to the pot, puts in a tin and lifts out some broth. He walks towards the child raising the tin to his nose. He smells it and throws it away in disgust.) Damn! — Damn!

(Enter Mr. Burns with a policeman)

Burns: There he is officer, just like I told you. (Tim whips around with fright and cowers towards the tent)

Policeman: (Taking a book and pencil from his pocket) Is your name Tim Casey?

Tim: (Fearfully) Yes, your honour.

Policeman: Then pack up and get moving. You know you are breaking the law.

Tim: Law, sir? What law? —

Policeman: You are camped on private property against the owner's wishes and you have been warned.

Tim: But — but I'm doing no harm, sir. I can't move. — The – the child is very sick. (Moving towards the tent) Look, sir. Look! It would be his death to move him now.

131

Policeman: That is not my concern. This man has lodged a complaint. You must move from his property. This land is private.

Tim: (Gaining a little courage) Can I camp by the road, then? On that patch at the corner?

Policeman: No. That is state property. You must keep moving.

Tim: Keep moving? — Can I not stop at all, sir?

Policeman: No. You must keep moving.

Tim: But how can I keep moving, sir? – Shur, I must stop somewhere?

Policeman: f you stop you constitute an obstruction and are subject to the penalty of the law. Pack up your bags now and move on, like a good man. We want no fuss here.

Tim: But what about the child, sir – He could – he could die, if I tried to shift him now.

Policeman: I'm afraid that is outside the law.

Tim: But — but — Sir!

Burns: Come on, Tim Casey. No more of your shenanagins! Get moving or it's arrested you'll be, and it's no more than you would deserve, you dirty vermin. Breaking down me ditches and defiling me land. Get your back out of here and never let me see you again.

(Tim hesitates)

Policeman: (Opening his book ominously) If you don't obey the orders I will have to arrest you.

Tim: (Quickly, with terror in his voice) Yes, sir! Yes, sir! (He starts gathering up the harness hurriedly)

(Enter Bridget, half pulling the priest behind her)

Priest: Let me go, woman! Let me go! Do you want me to call the wrath of God down upon you!

Bridget: But see for yourself, father! I'm not lying. As God is my honour —

Priest: Honour, Bridget Casey! What would you know about honour, — or God for that matter? You are a scourge on the country, the lot of you. Always up to some mischief.

Bridget: But it's only two pounds, father. Two pounds!

Priest: If I were to give two pounds to every lying tinker who comes the way with a sad story, I'd soon be on the road myself. (To Burns and the policeman) Hello, John — Pat. Are these ones giving you trouble?

Burns: There's no good talking to them, father. They have me plagued out of this world. But I'm putting a stop to it this time. (Indicating the policeman) If they don't get moving it's in gaol they'll be.

Bridget: But, Mr. Burns, we need help. (To the priest) For the mercy of God, father, we need help! Our only child is dying —

Priest: You will have to learn, Bridget Casey, to respect other people's property and not be causing a nuisance. People have enough trouble of their own without you plaguing them.

Policeman: They are causing an obstruction—(Looking at his book) contrary to paragraph nine, sub-section three, of the state by-laws.

Priest: Go on now, like decent folk and cause no more trouble, or the officer will have to take you in.

Tim: But what about the child, father? He's not fit to walk.

Priest: Well, it's to the authorities you should go if your child is not well. They'll see to you and get you a house. You shouldn't have a child walking the roads anyway.

Tim: But we were born to the roads, father. We couldn't live in a house. We couldn't have our bones crushed up between four walls —

Priest: (Angrily) I tell you it's not natural. God never intended people to walk the roads. He meant every man to have a roof over his head.

Tim: (Quietly) And is there a roof on heaven, father? Did God not make the stars and the fields and the sky —

Bridget: (Frantically, to Tim) Enough of this talk! What does that matter now? It's food we need and medicine. (She confronts the three who are standing in a row. Tim moves to the tent and stoops down beside the child.) Will no one help us? — Will you help me, father? For the love of God and his holy mother –two pounds!

Priest: (Angrily) Didn't I tell you already, you hussy, that I haven't got two pounds for you! Do you want me to put the curse of God upon you, you heathen! (Bridget moves to the policeman and makes a gesture to him)

Policeman: My job is to enforce the law, mam.

Bridget: (Moving to Burns) And will you help me, sir? You have children of your own —

Burns: Help you! I'll roast you, Bridget Casey, if you don't get moving this minute! Get your rags gathered and get on the road. Let the two of you and your child be stepping out this minute. There's no room for you here.

Tim: (Looking up slowly from the tent) The child won't be stepping out. He'll never be stepping out again — Bridget Casey, our child is dead.

(A hush falls. The other characters stand motionless.)

Bridget: (Walking slowly in awe to the tent) Dead, you say — dead? Then it's dead I am myself, Tim Casey. (She lifts the child and hugs it to her.) Oh, a mhuirnín (Vuirneen). A mhuirnín — My child — My son.

(The three shuffle their feet awkwardly)

Tim: Settle yourself, Bridget. Crying won't help him now. It was too much for him - the disease - the hunger. (Breaks down)

Bridget: (In a numbed quietness) Aye, a disease for which there is no cure, Tim Casey. The disease of poverty.

Burns: (Awkwardly) Ah — hem — Yous can stay till the morning. I'm — I'm sorry for the child.

Policeman: The – eh – the order will be rescinded until the morning. You can stay until you have the child —until — you have this matter cleared up.

Priest: I'll say a mass for him in the morning.

Bridget: (Blankly) But I have no money to give you, father. (The priest looks at her for a moment, then walks to the tent, taking the ribbon from his pocket and putting it around his neck.)

Tim: (Not catching Bridget's meaning) Don't be worrying about money now, woman. (He takes her by the shoulders and gently lifts her back.) Money is no good to us now. We'll get enough to do us along the road —

Bridget: It's a long road it'll be now — a long road in future from to-day until tomorrow with only the darkness of death upon it.

(The priest kneels beside the child and starts to give it the last rites.)

Tim: Somewhere there'll be a road with light on it – and – and pity.

Bridget: Pity, Tim Casey. That'll be the longest road of all, I'm thinking — the road that you and I will never go. (As the priest finishes the anointing they go on their knees.

Priest: In the name of the Father, and of the Son, and of the Holy Ghost. (The policeman and Burns hesitate, then join them awkwardly.) Oh, my God, I am heartily sorry for having offended thee —

CURTAIN

The Gypsies with their roadside tents are long gone. Gone also are the customs and aspects of life outlined in the preceding pages. The people who practiced them are also long gone.

135

* * *

I felt it appropriate to include some reference to the legends and mythology of the area. I also include a brief outline of two men who had a major impact on the lives of the people and community centuries ago, namely Art McCooey and Dr Patrick Donnelly.

Finally, I include a collection of unpublished poems – Undug Rigs.

Pathways of the Sun

(Legends & Pagan influences in The Ring of Gullion)

This part of South-East Ulster is home to many different legends. They have their origins in a distant past and provide one of the earliest insights we have into the mindset of the pre-Christian inhabitants of the Ring of Gullion area. At their centre is a cult of pagan mysticism that characterises much of the early literature of Ireland. From this were fashioned God-like figures of heroic stature that mirrored the terrain in which they were set. This is particularly so in the Ring of Gullion, from which walk figures as large and as timeless as the rock-strewn escarpment of hills and mountains which form so much of its landscape. They mirror a poetic imagination and romantic escapism rooted deep in our Celtic, and pre-Celtic, consciousness from the earliest times.

The Celts were strong believers in the supernatural, especially in the pagan Gods that ruled their lives – the Gods of the seasons, the land, fertility,— the very things on which they depended for their survival in their nomadic lifestyle. When they arrived in Ireland they found a people of a similar, but even more advanced, disposition, with a long established culture of Pagan worship and ritual, centred around skills and craftsmanship more advanced than anything they had encountered before. These native dwellers were to become for the Celts a matrix around which they wove many of the great legends that form the nucleus of early Irish literature. In them their fertile imagination and other-world beliefs could find their ultimate fulfilment.

The two greatest folk heroes run from the mould of this pagan mysticism in Ireland are Cuchulainn and Finn Mac Cool. They form the subject matter of two of the country's four Cycles of Literature, the Rúraíocht and the Fiannaíocht. Both of them are closely linked to this landscape of the Ring of Gullion.

Cuchulainn in particular dominates the early literature and folklore of this area and is the genesis of much of its later folk consciousness, perhaps even to modern times. Through various stages of its history this part of South-

East Ulster has been known under different distinguishing titles, especially during the great age of its 18th century poets, but more than anything else it was, and still remains, Cuchulainn Country. In him is enshrined the timeless symbolism inherent in this landscape.

What more fitting setting could there be for Ulster's greatest hero, for his transformation from human to superhuman, than Slieve Gullion, the highest prominence in this whole area of South-East Ulster? This mountain was imbued with the same grandeur of stature, and indomitable spirit that the hero himself would later assume.

The setting for Cuchulainn's birth was just south of the Ring of Gullion in the plain of Muirtheimhne, at Dealga Fort, after which the present town of Dún Dealgan, Dundalk, is named. The story of his life and exploits links North Louth and South-East Ulster, as they were historically linked in early times, this part of Louth still being part of the Province of Ulster.

The Ring of Gullion acts as a passageway, through which this story moves to and fro between Dealga Fort and the ancient city of Eamhain Macha, present day Navan Fort, which was the royal seat of the then High King of Ireland, Conor Mac Neasa.

Cuchulainn's childhood name was Séadanda, better known in English as Setanta. He was born of illustrious parentage. His father, Sualdamh according to the more traditional version of his origin, was a Taoiseach, or Chieftain, in North-Louth, a position of power and high social ranking. He quite clearly lived in a style that matched his status, judging from the distinctive nature of his fortress home, the site of which still stands a short distance from Dún Lughaidh castle, the present day St. Louis' Secondary School just off the Castletown road in Dundalk. His mother, Deichtíre, was the sister of the High King himself, Conor Mac Neasa.

According to a custom which was very prevalent in early Ireland, as is indicated by the numerous references to it in legends, known as Altram (Fosterage), it was only a matter of time before the young Séadanda would be setting out to his uncle's castle in Eamhain Macha. This was a tradition whereby children who had illustrious relatives were sent at a fairly early age to the homes of those relatives to be raised, and tutored in the social graces and military arts, as would befit their Clan status.

When still no more than a child we see the young hero setting out alone, despite his mother's protestations, down through the Ring of Gullion on his long journey to his uncle's castle.

Shortly after his arrival a party was being given for Conor Mac Neasa and members of his court by Culann, the chief blacksmith attached to his castle. It was at this party that the young lad was to undergo his metamorphosis from human to superhuman when he killed the fierce hound of Culann. This was reputedly the largest and fiercest wolfhound in Ireland which no warrior had ever been able to pass. He was the only protection that Culann had ever needed for his castle, even on such an occasion as this when the High-King of Ireland was present.

When Séadanda arrived late at the party and the hound who had been let loose in the yard came to devour him, as he had done with others, the young lad struck his hurley ball with his camán, both of which he always carried with him, down his throat and "out his body", a feat which for a lad of his age was a presage of the superhuman prowess he would later display.

In an attempt to appease Culann who was very distressed at the loss of the hound, Séadanda told him that he would scour Ireland to find a pup of the same breed and that he would raise and train him until he would be fit to replace the hound he had killed. In the meantime he said that he would take the place of the hound and guard his castle.

The pagan soothsayer, Cathbad, who was present spoke up and said,

"'Tis well you have spoken. From this day forth you will be known as Cú Chulainn, The Hound Of Culann, a name which will soon be known throughout the length and breadth of Ireland." This event, which marks Séadanda's first step across the threshold from his human to his later divine form, occurred on the top of Sliabh gCuilinn, Slieve Gullion, which derives its name from the blacksmith.

The greatest legend of all concerning Cuchulainn, where we see the words of Cathbad being fulfilled, is the Táin Bó Chuailnge, the Cattle Raid of Cooley. It is here that we see Cuchulainn achieving his final God-like status.

It was before his contest with Lóch that the Goddess of war, the Morrígan, (i.e. the Mór-Ríoghan – the Great Queen) came to Cuchulainn. She healed his wounds after the battle and remained with him from then on, assisting him. It was also, very significantly, before the great carnage at Knockbridge that Cuchulainn was visited by the God Lugh, who told him that he was his father from the Sí, the Fairy Host, and that he had come to assist him. He stood guard while Cuchulainn slept and regained his strength.

During this slaughter a graphic description is given of the battle fury, or "riastradh", that Cuchulainn experienced from his early childhood. The change that comes over him is not just one of spirit but also a major physical one. His whole body changes until he takes on the appearance of an invincible, primeval dragon, with distended head and snapping jaws. During the course of the battle he himself, just like the Sí, was completely invisible to the enemy. After this great slaughter Ailill estimated that almost half of the 54,000 warriors they had set out with, had been slain along the way by Cuchulainn. Throughout the Táin Epic Cuchulainn performs deeds equal to that of a whole army. In him is personified the might of Ulster, which stands God-like and omnipotent. Through him the roots of Ulster's early history are seen to be set firmly in the cult of the Divine, a cult to which the man from whom he derived his name, Culann, is also linked.

There has always been a certain mystique surrounding Culann. Folk memory seems to have allowed him to cross time barriers and he figures in legends set many centuries apart. The key is to be found in the story concerning the early life of Cuchulainn, where it is said that, not only was Culann the most skilled blacksmith in Ulster at that time, but his skill was such that he had actually been in service with the famed Tuatha Dé Danann, the name given in legend to the people who occupied Ireland at the time of the arrival of the Celts.

These people, the Tuatha Dé Danann, as we have said, had a very strong influence on our Celtic ancestors. They are the originators of all things mystical, magical, and otherworldly in Irish folklore from those early times down to the present day. Their presence occupied the shadow lands of tales about fairies, ghosts, and the Banshee (Bean Sí – Fairy Woman) around the fireside at night in the Céilí Houses during my youth. It is they, more than any other, who lie at the heart of virtually all the stories associated with the Ring of Gullion area. Their name means The Followers of the Goddess Dana.

The name Dana is a later corruption by early scholars of the original Gaelic form Ana (or Anu), the mythological Goddess of abundance, the mother of the Earth. She was considered by tenth century scholars to be the originator of all the Gods of Irish Mythology.

These people were of the same race as the Firbolg, the tribe who preceded them in Ireland, both having their origins in Greece, but they were of a completely different character to their distant cousins. Whereas the Firbolg were a warlike race who exerted their influence by Treise Lámh (physical power), with very little social graces or cultural distinction associated with them, the Tuatha Dé Danann come across in early legends as people of outstanding cultural qualities, possessing a wide range of skills in artistry, many of which the Celts had never before seen. They are always depicted as friends of the earth and of man, with highly accomplished skills in instrument making, music, ornamentation, lacework, and, especially, the working of gold. The Celts, although fighting against them, had an enormous respect for them, which later manifested itself in a number of forms in early legends. They were raised to the level of the supernatural, which set them outside of time, just like Culann himself. Another legend here in the Ring of Gullion suggests, as we shall see in a moment, that Culann not only worked for them but was actually a member of their race, thus explaining his outstanding ability.

This story has in it the seeds of other legends, which evolved in folklore concerning this ancient race, which show the early Celtic reverence for them. Not wishing to accept that they had disappeared entirely, two beliefs sprang up concerning them. The first was that they had only gone a short distance away, to some magic Isle just off the coast of Ireland. Since the Celts wanted to remember them just as they were, this had to be a place where nothing ever changed, the Land of Eternal Youth – Tír Na nÓg. This theme was developed at some length and to great effect in the story concerning the son of the later legendary hero, Finn Mc Cool, the leader of the Fianna. This is a story of rare escapist beauty, which tells the tale of Niamh of the Golden Hair, the Queen of Tír Na nÓg, coming back to Ireland to carry off Finn's son, Oisín, to this mystical land. This has found its way into modern literature in many haunting forms, not only in poetry, but even in the more popular medium of film, in the story "Into The West".

The second belief that sprang up is a logical development of the above – They have not left at all. They are still here. Well, if they are, how is it that we don't see them? – They are very small. And where do they live? They live underground – The origin of the Slua Sí, the Fairies, which to this day are always referred to in Irish as Na Daoine Maithe, the good people.

It is clear from the stories associated with the Ring of Gullion that the Tuatha Dé Danann have left an indelible mark here. It is they who have fashioned most of the legends in this area, including those concerning Cuchulainn, as we shall see shortly. It is a presence that still lurks in the background even in modern times.

During my childhood in Lislea our parents always warned us, especially at Easter time, when we all headed for Slieve Gullion, never on any account to go near the lake on the top of the mountain. If we did, our hair would turn grey. This I believed firmly for many years. I was surprised later to find its origins lurking in a tale contained amongst the legends in Laoithe Na Féinne, the Lays of the Fianna. The tale goes under two titles, Toraíocht Shliabh gCuilinn (The Pursuit of Slieve Gullion), and Laoi Na Seilge (The Lay of the Hunt).

This was one of the whole cycle of tales told to St. Patrick by Oisín, when he returned from Tír Na nÓg after an absence of three hundred years. Although the Fianna lived during the High-Kingship of Cormac Mac Airt, some two centuries later than Conor Mac Neasa, Culann still looms large in this story.

In it we are told that Culann had two daughters, both of whom were in love with Finn Mc Cool, then a dashing young hero. One of them was under a geasa, a bond, whereby she could never have anything to do with an older man. The other, wishing to gain an advantage over her, used the magical powers of her Sí ancestry and turned herself into a deer and headed for Mt. Almhain in Kildare, the main residence of the Fianna. Finn and his two dogs Bran and Sceolang were out for a stroll, taking a break from a period of feasting that was in progress. The deer presented herself before them on the nearby hill, almost inviting capture.

As soon as the hounds caught sight of the deer they took off after it, with Finn at their heels. The pursuit continued the whole way from Kildare down through Naas, Dublin, Drogheda, through the Muirtheimhne plain and Dundalk, until they finally arrived at the top of Slieve Gullion. At this point the deer disappeared.

As Finn stood scratching his head in amazement, for never before had any four-legged creature been able to outrun himself and his two hounds, he heard a sound as of a woman crying. When he went to investigate he found a beautiful young maiden sitting on the bank of the lake on the summit of Slieve Gullion weeping profusely. She told him that a gold ring she had on her finger had fallen off into the water of the lake. She put him as a warrior of the Fianna under a geasa to retrieve it for her. Finn stripped off his clothes and dived into the lake. On the fifth attempt he found the ring and headed back to the bank. As he swam the maiden cast a spell on the lake waters and before Finn had his feet planted firmly on dry ground he was turned into a withered, grey-haired, feeble old man, with scarcely the strength to stand. The maiden grabbed the ring and disappeared.

Eventually the other members of the Fianna, having followed the tracks of the chase, arrived at the top of Slieve Gullion. Finn at first was ashamed to tell them that he, now a wizened old man, was their heroic leader. Later that night he confided to Caoilte Mac Rónáin what had happened. The Fianna were outraged at such a deed being done to their leader, an insult to all the Fianna. They swore revenge. Placing their shields carefully under Finn, they raised him on their shoulders and carried him "Northwards" from the lake until they reached Culann's castle.

The castle was underground in a Sidh, a fairy mound. They called on Culann to come out and answer for his daughter's treachery. Culann refused, so the Fianna began to dig into the Sidh:

Seven days without respite
The troop dug into the Sidh
Until suddenly Culann came
Out before us from his cave.

In his hand we discerned
A golden goblet full of wine
Which he gave to the Fianna king
Lying prostrate on the hill.

Finn drank without delay
The fairy quaff in his hand
And to his form again returned
Finn the king, but grey of hair.

This is clearly the origin of the warning our parents used give us in childhood. It surprised me that the echo of this legend should still remain in Lislea down to modern times. It was first written down from folk memory in the fifteenth century and had existed in oral tradition for many centuries previously. This is only one of many examples that one could quote that would suggest that primeval mythical influences, rooted deep in a distant and pagan past, still exert a strong influence on the modern Christian consciousness of this area, as they do in many other places in Ireland.

Who of us, for example, could claim not to have broken at least one of the Ten Commandments? But who of us here in the Ring of Gullion would take a saw, or an axe, and go out and cut a lone fairy bush in the middle of a field? Indeed, there are examples in recent times of major construction works being halted, such as in the Fairy Glen in Newry some years ago, because of the existence of such a bush where no one could be found willing to remove it.

The Tuatha Dé Danann are still clearly close at hand, hovering in our consciousness here in the shadow of Slieve Gullion, as they are in the above Fianna legend. There is no doubt that in this story Culann with his magical powers, and those of his daughter, is indicated as being a member of this race. In the original story concerning Cuchulainn fighting the hound, his castle is seen as a normal, regular castle with its courtyard, but here it disappears underground and can only be approached through the Sidh, the fairy mound.

In local tradition Culann's daughter still haunts Slieve Gullion in the form of the Cailleach Beara, the legendary witch who resides on the mountain. Her presence still hovers in the air here and the geasa concerning her lake still exerts an influence on our minds, as we have seen above. I myself have found this to be true even in recent times.

A few years ago I was asked to lead a group of people up the mountain, a mixture of both locals and strangers, who were attending a festival in Tí Chulainn Cultural Centre in Mullaghbawn. As we wound our way upward I told them the story of the mountain, much as I have done here. Along the way I added, with a straight face, that the spell on the lake had been reversed in recent years by Cardinal Tomas Ó Fiaich R.I.P., and that now anyone who bathed his head in its waters would have his hair restored to its former glory.

Some time later when we reached the top of the mountain and I was telling the story of the Cairns, I noticed something out of the corner of my eye. When I turned round I saw that two elderly gentlemen had removed themselves from the group and were over at the other side of the lake where the bank was low. They were both down on their knees dipping their bald heads into the lake water. Such is the pagan faith still strong amongst us!

This shadowy presence of the Tuatha Dé Danann has woven its way not only into the stories of the Ring of Gullion, but also into the mindset and traditions of the area. It is only when we understand this that a lot of the legends here begin to make sense, including those concerning Cuchulainn.

Of the two traditions relating to the Tuatha Dé Danann it is clearly the second one that was the most prevalent in this area from the earliest times, namely, that they are still here in the invisible, magical form of the Sí. Many of our legends, place names, traditions, and even physical structures are part of an ancient pagan homage to them, lodged now in the subconscious. The name of my own area, Lislea, has a direct linkage to them.

Lios is one of the earliest words in Irish for a dwelling place. When the Celts first came to Ireland they continued the nomadic traditions which they had followed in Europe. The only time during the year that they settled down was in winter, when they built a circular fortified camp, inside which all the animals were taken. The name for this winter camp was Lios.

The highlight of the year was, Bealtaine, May Day, when all the animals were released and they continued on their nomadic trail. Many rituals were performed on this day, including the carrying of lit torches around the camp, the reciting of ritual incantations, and the lighting of two fires in close proximity, between which the animals were driven to be purified by the smoke – Idir dhá thine Bhealtaine, between two May fires.

It was believed that the Tuatha Dé Danann in their Sí form visited each Lios during these rituals and performed their own unseen, but equally important, magic rites to impart good fortune and fertility for the coming year. They represented the spirit of the land, the Good People. Their association with the Lios has caused the meaning of this word to change to the present day "Fairy Fort".

There were many God-leaders associated with the Tuatha Dé Danann – Lear the God of the sea, Aonghus the God of love, Brighit the Goddess of the countryside, Lugh the God of fertility and genius. Virtually all the male figures in the long list are said to have been fathered by the Daghda, the supreme God of all the Tuatha Dé Danann, a distant figure who hovers in the background of many legends.

If you look closely at his name you can see, perhaps, the origin of the folk concept concerning the Tuatha Dé Danann. His name is a compound word, the first part of which, "dagh", is a very old prefix in Irish. In my youth the spelling had changed to "deagh", and it has now been shortened to "dea". It means "good". The second part, -da, is the old spelling of the modern word dia, meaning God. So, the name means the "Good God", hence the term the "Good People", and the great respect shown to them by the ordinary people.

In addition to this, the greatest of all the Daghda's sons was Lugh. Whereas others were Gods of individual parts of the earth, — sea, rivers, mountains etc., Lugh was God of everything, the sea, the land, the sky, and, indeed, life itself – a unified deity. It is thought today that this is the reason for St. Patrick's success in spreading Christianity so quickly in Ireland. The concept of a single deity had already been laid in pagan belief. It was simply a matter of superimposing the new Christian concept on the original pagan one.

Evidence of this strange betrothal can still be seen today in many places in Ireland, including the Ring of Gullion, where the partners still walk hand in hand in rituals that interlink both pagan and Christian practices in a neat balance. The key is nearly always the God Lugh.

The first great battle that Lugh fought was against the Sun. Lugh defeated the Sun and took its place, the God of life, earth, and all living things.

The circular shape of the early Lios was not an accident. It was constructed deliberately in homage to the Sun. All the rituals carried out on May Day followed the path of the Sun, clockwise around the Lios. Ancient burial mounds, including two on Slieve Gullion, were built in the same circular shape. So too are stone mounds associated with Christianity, where pilgrims still walk the pathway of the Sun around them, as on Lough Derg and Croke Patrick.

In the case of the latter, people walk today around stone mounds, the supposed burial place of saints, some of which pre-date Christianity by two millennia. This mountain was one of the great pagan centres of Ireland, dominating the local area both physically and symbolically, a fact whose significance was not lost on St. Patrick. He wasted little time in claiming it for Christianity and stamping the new Christian imprint on the old pagan image, but the original still shimmers through the overlay.

This is also true in the case of the pagan Goddess Brighit. Her later Christian form rose, almost from the shingle of Slieve Gullion, at Faughart, St. Brigid. The devotion to her and the many ceremonies performed in her honour eclipsed the memory of her pagan counterpart, but not quite. St. Brigid's feast day, which still falls significantly at Imbolc, the ancient pagan feast celebrating the first day of Spring, the first of February, is a gentle reminder of her presence. So too is the culture of the stones associated with the Saint's birthplace, and the much revered St. Brigid's cross, always hung in byres and outhouses during my youth to protect the animals, which reflects in its structure the rays of the sun. We see it also in the dances taught to schoolchildren to be performed in her honour on her feast day, in fact, ritual dances of fertility.

Today flowers, which were always scattered on May Day in honour of the Tuatha Dé Danann, or Sí, the guardians of the land, around doorsteps and on byre roofs, are now placed in honour of the Blessed Virgin. So too the May fires, lit now under a Christian guise, so that the old phrase, Idir dhá thine Bhealtaine, between two May fires, has taken on a new meaning in Irish, "on the horns of a dilemma", torn between the pagan and the Christian in ourselves.

The Druids were the first to shave their heads in a circle in homage to Lugh, the Sun-God. This custom was later adopted by Irish monks. It found its way into ancient stone engravings of the pagan era, where variations of the circular form is the most common feature. It transferred from there into Christian symbolism, as seen in Celtic Crosses, and into calligraphy in the illuminated manuscripts of the early Christian era, the most notable being the Book of Kells.

An excellent example of the combination of both of these in this area is seen in the famous stone of Killnasagart. This stone, the earliest inscribed Christian memorial in Ireland, stands just a few hundred yards below Moyry Castle in the Gap of The North. It was inscribed with its Christian motifs in the year 714 A.D., by Ternoc, son of Ciaran the Small, and dedicated to Saint Peter. The stone, however, has stood there much longer than that. It was, in fact, an ancient druidic memorial, marking a pagan burial site. The new Christian inscription was superimposed on the original pagan symbolism of circles and Ogham writing. A fairly sizeable portion of the right corner of the stone has been chiselled away where the main part of the Ogham inscription stood, (the remains of the Ogham can still be seen clearly at the back of the stone) and crosses carved in its place, still set inside the ritual pagan circles. These seem here, as in the manuscripts and Celtic crosses, to have been given a new Christian interpretation, — the circle of truth, light, eternity etc. Or, as some suggest, in a rare convolution, the triumph of Christianity over Paganism.

I have already said that in some stories in mythology it is suggested that Sualdamh is not Cuchulainn's father, but rather the great God Lugh himself. Clear evidence of this is given in the Táin, with the appearance of Lugh at Cuchulainn's side before the great carnage, his statement to him that he was his father from the Sí (the Tuatha Dé Danann), and his assurances for his safety in the battle. It is clear that it is from Lugh that Cuchulainn inherited the superhuman powers which he possessed.

This presence of the Sí runs through the Táin. Its influence is seen even amongst the Connacht forces when Meave's charioteer turns her chariot in a circle to the right following the path of the Sun, before they left Cruachain, to invoke good fortune for a safe return. We see it also in the case of the Goddess of war, the Morrígan who assisted Cuchulainn.

If we turn to the Ring of Gullion area we can see a lot of these influences coming together, and begin to understand the part this area played in this whole culture of the Tuatha Dé Danann, which lies at the centre of so many of its legends.

It is from the God Lugh that County Louth derives its name, Condae Lú. It is there that he was born, the son of Eithne, a leader of a branch of the Tuatha De Danann from Connacht, and Cian, the man who gave his name to Killen Hill, the place where his son Lugh buried him after he was killed by the three sons of Tuireann.

According to Eoghan Ó Camhraí, one of the compilers of the Annals of the Four Masters, Dealga Fort itself, where Cuchulainn was born, derived its name from Delga, an ancient warrior of the tribal cousins of the Tuatha Dé Danann, the Firbolg. This explains the form Dealgan (i.e. "of Delga") in the genitive singular in the name Dún Dealgan. In Mythology, we know that Cuchulainn's Divine father, Lugh, had close blood ties with the Fir Bolg, being fostered in youth with one of their famous female warriors, Tailte. It was at the place named after her that the last great battle was fought between the Tuatha Dé Danann and the Celts, Cath Thailteann, the Battle of Teltown, in County Meath.

If we move a short distance down the Ring of Gullion we find one of the forts of the Tuatha Dé Danann, the Lios of my own area, Lislea (Lios Liath). It is not, perhaps, without significance that we have another townland of the same name in the vicinity of Dealga Fort, and one beside Eamhain Macha, the home of Cuchulainn's uncle.

Towering in the centre of this area, the highest point of all, is the great mountain of Slieve Gullion, the place where Lugh's son was given his name, rising directly above this Lios. If we climb to its summit once more and look around at the clear circle of hills which form the Ring Dyke, we might well be forgiven for thinking that nature itself has got in on the act, the greatest symbolic shrine of all, one could say, to the God Lugh, the massive circular mound of the Ring of Gullion. This is almost a mirror image of the circle of the Sun, engraved indelibly into the earth in this ring of mountain tops. Such a symbolic setting was the obvious place to select for the consecration of the God Lugh's son, Cuchulainn, into his heroic form, held aloft in the arms of Slieve Gullion, the altar of the Gods. It was appropriate also that it was in this area that his greatest battles should have been fought, fulfilling the promise of his childhood, first shown on this mountain.

The Ring of Gullion and the area at the centre of which it stands is inlaid with the symbolism of this ancient pagan mysticism, which has seeded itself into many legends, and into numerous figures who have been formed inside its womb, both in Mythology and, even, in modern history.

Here beneath the shades of Lugh's people we walk, along a marginal line between pagan fantasy and modern reality, embracing a new Christian world, with our pagan past still at our back.

Finally, one of the most surprising places where this ancient homage to Lugh is still found alive and flourishing, out in the open, is in a tradition that has come in recent years to symbolise the spirit of Ireland itself, Irish dancing. The wheeling, circular formations which run as a vein throughout its movements are an echo of the ancient pagan ritual dance in honour of Lugh. This is especially true in reels where it is most evident.

The swinging circles follow the path of the Sun in this timeless ritual of fertility, a celebration of life itself. Today, breaking free from the formal restrictions of Christian mores placed upon it, it has danced, rejoicing, into the liberated freedom of River Dance.

I had occasion recently to have this brought home to me during the course of a family wedding, which I had been asked to record on video. In the process of making copies of it I was watching, again and again, this weaving, wheeling movement of the dance as performed by a local group of Irish dancers. It came to assume an almost hypnotic form, drawing me closer and closer to it, until I was carried back through time to its rhythm. It beat its way to the dances held in the houses in this area in my youth, to the rusted tin hall in Lislea, and to the old type weddings, which were always held at home, where the celebrations went on all day and throughout the night. The barns, cleaned out of the hay, straw, and instruments with which they had been cluttered all year, suddenly became new, exciting places, the arenas of this ancient fertility ritual, their floors glistening to the polished sheen of candle wax. Women, whom we may last have seen in their traditional smocks, feeding the hens or giving hay to the cows, were transformed with a new, unbelievable beauty, into rhythmic, sensuous forms. They weaved their way across the floor, lost in the rhythm of the dance, stirring young men to begin to dream new, and oftimes impossible dreams. They danced to the beat of time back through Brighit, the pagan Goddess of fertility, through Anu, back to the Garden of Eden itself, to the most celebrated temptress of them all, Eve.

DANCING

She danced before us in the moonlight,
In her eyes the fire of sun,
As on a forest floor she danced

Where ancient wars were won.
Her dancing feet wove patterns
That rhythmed her from dancehall
Into naked stone,
Where she danced in hieroglyphics,
Through Ogham and Celtic crosses,
Along lines once chiselled finely
In the sculpture of man's timing;

Through the Book of Kells and Leinster
To where I found her
In barns swept clean for passion
Of hay and barrels standing,
Where she danced to ancient twinings
Of the harp strings and the lyre,
On fiddles played by maestros
Of notes long stored in hillsides,
In the staff of rock and cradle,
On fingers plucked, long chiselled
To the lines of their refinement,

Where she weaved and danced
Till dawn's bright sun was shining
Through oak beams cracked
Which cast her naked shadow
On walls where halters hung
In tune with bridle bit and britching;
nd young men wove their dreams
Around her naked image
In fields of Summer where the scythes
Through corn and wheat were swinging,
And their hearts were dancing
Tunes of joy and sorrow
On foot rigs where their hopes were glimpsed
In fleeting shadows
Through gaps in walls, barns, and in cabins,

Of the day that they would twine
Their arms around her naked body
And dance in moonlight
Till their hearts were burning,
As on a forest floor they danced
Beneath the fire of summer.

Art McCooey

The seventeenth century marks the period of greatest change in the social history of Ireland. By the time it ended the structure of Irish society, which had existed for centuries, would be changed utterly. The great Irish Earls, the ruling aristocracy who represented the backbone of the country, were now gone. They were either killed in one or other of the three risings in that century or banished from the country, with their lands confiscated, in the three stages of Plantation which resulted as a consequence of those risings. The peasant class was left without leaders and the poets were left without patrons.

From the earliest times poetry was one of the most influential, and most profitable, professions in Ireland. Every large house traditionally had a body of poets attached to it whose job it was to record, and celebrate, the main events in the life of the household. They were also charged with keeping a precise record of the ever-expanding genealogy of the earldom.

At that time, according to Irish, or Breton, law the position of Earl did not pass down automatically from father to son. Everyone inside five generations of relationship had an equal claim to the succession. These people were known as Rithe Damhna, or Heirs Apparent, a position which granted them a very high social ranking, much the same as minor royals today. In order for these people to maintain their status exactitude in the genealogical table was essential. This was also the case after a succession if the inheritance swung to the left or right of the genealogical centre. A number of people would suddenly find themselves included in the new lineage of inheritance and would move from unknown figures to the top of the social class. A comparable group on the other side would just as suddenly find themselves deprived of their privileged status and be relegated to obscurity.

These poets were also the custodians of the vast body of literature, both verse and prose, of early Ireland, which was preserved entirely inside the oral tradition. One of the major tasks of the poets was to commit this literature to memory and be prepared to deliver any part of it when required. For example, at any large gathering in the house of an Earl at which a poet was in attendance anyone present had the right to call upon him to recite a named piece of poetry or to recount a particular lay. If he couldn't do so he would be in disgrace and his career would be at an end.

Such feats of memory were matched only by the poets' own compositions. The poetry which they composed is known as Syllabic Poetry. This was an extremely intricate form of composition which was governed by numerous rules as regards metrical format and syntactical agreement between a large number of vowel and consonantal groupings. The rules were such that one often wonders how they managed to compose anything inside their rigid strictures. It is accepted today that the early poetry of Ireland was among the most intricate and most intellectual of all the early poetry of Europe. It is little wonder, therefore, that these poets were full-time, professional men whose lives were devoted entirely to scholarship.

The poets were held in high regard and wielded a level of power which was often second only to the Earls themselves. Whereas ordinary citizens had their movements strictly governed by tribal boundaries which they could cross only at their peril, no such restrictions applied to the poets. They were the only group of people in Ireland who could move freely and with impunity across all tribal boundaries. They were sacrosanct.

It was completely unheard of for anyone to molest a poet in any way or to show him discourtesy. Just as a praise poem written by a poet in honour of an Earl could bring the Earl great distinction, and the poet great riches, so also could the poet seriously undermine the reputation of the Earl if he were in any way aggrieved. This would be achieved by the poet using the most potent, and also the most feared, weapon in his armoury, the Satire, or Íor.

If an Earl were to earn the displeasure of a poet the latter could wreck vengeance on him by composing a blistering satire which could call himself and his whole household into ridicule. Because of the universality of the poetic infrastructure such a satire would spread immediately along the grapevine and would soon be recited in every large house in the country, to the great detriment of the Earl's reputation. A poet, therefore, was always shown the height of courtesy and hospitality in any household which he visited.

Through the course of the seventeenth century all this changed utterly. Starting with the first plantation in the early part of the century under James 1 the poets suddenly found themselves without patrons. The respective Earls disappeared almost at a stroke and their large houses were either pulled down or occupied by a new ascendancy who had no need whatsoever for the Poets' services and to whom neither the Poets' language nor their great volume of learning had any relevance whatsoever. Suddenly the poets were faced with an awful reality, one that had never ever been encountered before by such an elitist group — They would have to work for a living!

From here on poetry would never again be a fulltime professional occupation in Ireland but merely a part-time one. The poets had to learn new trades and become farmers, teachers, carpenters, labourers etc., something which they considered to be completely beneath them and their profession. This sense of indignity and fall from grace was still echoed by the poets of the next century, especially by Art McCooey.

Now that poetry had become a part-time occupation the rigorous format of the Syllabic metrical system would have to change. Such intricate form of composition with its numerous rules could only be practiced by those for whom it was a fulltime profession.

Side by side with Syllabic poetry there had always existed a poetic format used by untrained poets and balladeers called the Amhrán metre. The erudite bards would always have looked down on this with disdain as being completely beneath them. It was to this, however, that the new breed of poets now turned, but if they did they changed it utterly.

One of the great merits of the Amhrán metre was that it was based on the natural rhythm and flow of the language itself, not on external rules. The poets enriched it and embellished it and eventually turned it into the sweetest and most melodious form of poetic expression ever to come out of Ireland, a veritable symphony of sound. Today the poetry of the eighteenth century, the swan song of a dying era, is regarded as the golden age of Gaelic poetry.

By the end of the century, when the Earls, such as the great O'Neill clan from South Armagh who had been banished to Connacht by Cromwell, were finally expelled from the country under the third and final stage of the plantations, the Williamite Plantation, the only people left to act as a voice for the uneducated peasant class were the Gaelic poets. The strange thing is that in this great era of Gaelic poetry all the Ulster Poets, with the exception of Cathal Buí Mac Giolla Gunna from Cavan, came from South East Ulster, from the area known as the Fews. This name comes from the Irish word Feadha, meaning trees, and refers to the area covered by the expansive wood of Dunreavey, essentially most of South Armagh and North Louth. Of these one of the best loved, and best known in his lifetime, was Art McCooey, or Art Na gCeoltaí, Art of the songs, as the people called him.

Of all the poets of the eighteenth century Art McCooey was most keenly aware of the great honour and distinction afforded to the poets in times gone by. This was a stark contrast to his own day when poets, according to himself, were looked upon by the nobility at best with curiosity and at worst with disdain. He was constantly harking back to the days of Ireland's former glory, and especially the glory once enjoyed by South Armagh when the great O' Neill clan ruled there, with their stately castle standing tall and proud on the top of Glassdrummond height.

These O' Neills were a second branch of the legendary O' Neills of Tyrone who had headed south around the year 1450 to seek new territory under their young king Aodh Ó Néill. They drove out the local clans of the Murphys, the Hanrattys, and the Garveys and set up an expanding dynasty that was to last for two hundred years and dominate the society of the area.

During the first rebellion of the Earls in 1595, led by the head of the O' Neills of Tyrone, Hugh O' Neill, the leader of the O' Neills of South Armagh was Turlough Mac Henry O' Neill. Turlough was actually a half brother of the great Hugh, both of them sharing a common mother, Joan Maguire. Turlough supported Hugh during the rebellion and as a result won much praise from later poets, including Art McCooey. The praise, however, was somewhat misplaced because later history was to prove that Turlough had played a very shrewd and, considering the area in which he lived, a very dangerous game. Although ostensibly supporting his half brother, Hugh O' Neill, he was in collusion with the English right up to and including the Battle of Kinsale in 1601.

During the first Plantation, following the rebellion, while the O' Neills of Tyrone and the O' Donnells of Donegal and the other Northern chieftains who had rebelled were having their estates confiscated, Turlough Mac Henry was granted nine thousand acres of O' Neill land in the Upper Fews, and was also knighted "for services rendered to the crown."

It was at this time, when other large houses were being pulled down, that Turlough, now Sir Turlough Mac Henry, completed the last great castle of the O' Neills, commenced by his father Henry, on Glassdrummond height. It is said to have rivalled in splendour any of the dwellings being built by the new gentry. Life continued on here as before for almost a further half century, with the pomp, pageantry and splendour associated with such houses, and of course the long celebrated O' Neill patronage of poets. It is this, I think, more than anything else that explains why the tradition of poetry continued on in the Upper Fews into the next generation and why it is in this area that virtually all the eighteenth century Ulster poets are to be found.

The O' Neill glory days came to an end in the Fews after the second rebellion of 1641. In the later Cromwellian Plantation in 1654 they were hunted to Connacht and given six thousand acres of bog land in lieu of the nine thousand acres of rich land they had occupied in the Creggan area. After the battle of the Boyne in 1690 they lost even this and were expelled completely from the country during the Williamite Plantation. By the time

Art McCooey came on the scene the great castle of Glassdrummond was lying in ruins, with only a small portion of it still standding

Art was born in the small town land of Ballinaghy which lies just below Glassdrummond height, almost in sight of the ruins of the O' Neill castle. This was a constant reminder to him of the glory once enjoyed by the area, and especially the distinction once afforded to poets inside its walls, a theme that is common in his poetry.

Whereas other poets refer to Ireland, especially in their Aisling, or Vision, poems, McCooey always refers to the spirit of the O' Neills. To him the former greatness of the O' Neills equated with the greatness of his own homeland. In over half the poems and songs of Art that survive he mentions the O' Neills. It is clear that he entertained the forlorn hope that the O' Neills would somehow rise again and restore the area to its former glory, and the poets to their former level of distinction. The last of the O' Neills of the Fews in Art's time was Daniel O' Neill, a close friend of the poet's. Art placed all his hope in Daniel's son, Art Óg, a young, dashing, heroic figure who seems to have inherited all the qualities of the royal O' Neills of the past. McCooey felt sure that somehow he would reverse history and restore the ancient dynasty, with all its social trappings.

McCooey was the son of a small farmer who worked 22 acres of land. On his death, as was the custom of the time, his land was divided equally between his two sons, Art and Turlough. Art took his share and, like the proverbial Prodigal Son, squandered it very quickly. He spent the rest of his life as a wandering labourer, working very often as a gardener. This may have had the effect of bringing him closer to the ordinary people and causing him to be considered one of them. It may also account for the popularity of his compositions and for the great affection in which he was held. He was able to give voice to the feelings of the people, to their sufferings, their hatreds, their laments, and their hopes.

Although Art's poems still reflect much of the refinement of expression and grandness of poetical posture of the former era, they also contain a great deal of the colour of his own time when richness of voice and tone and fertility of imagination, coupled with incisiveness and biting satire, were still very much a feature of the South Armagh mentality. He reserves the most acerbic edge of his tongue for the Planters, the new aristocracy of his day, referring to them often as Clann Bhullaigh, John Bull's people, or Clann Liútair, Luther's people. Quite a lot can be learned from his compositions about the traumatic changes in society which were happening before him and particularly the changes in the lot of the peasant class.

There was now a major difference between the new overlords and the native Gaels. "Wully and Jane" can get leases, but Catholics cannot get a freehold, nor vote, nor carry arms. The Big House was now occupied by the Clann Liútair, while the peasants were confined to "a smoky cabin with a cow". Also the natives had to walk, while Luther's People travelled in coaches decked out in style, the man with his hat "embellished with a cross-cockade, and his wife with

> " — Her fine hat and its golden band
> And a feather ploughing in the wind."

In another place we see the rich woman decked out in "silk and satin, straining herself in her lace" while the peasant woman "hadn't a stitch on her knees or a buckle on her boot."

The repressive society of the day was personified for McCooey and for many others in the person of John Johnston, or Johnston of the Fews as he is normally referred to. Johnston was appointed chief constable of the Fews in the year 1710, with the special task of hunting down members of the underground movement, known at that time as the Tories, later to be called the Rapparees. Since the law of the day stated that anyone in such a position of authority could summarily behead anyone whom they captured and suspected of being a Tory, without any further proof being required, Johnston was given very wide remit. He has gone down in history with a large degree of infamy. No one was safe from his hand, not only the outlaws, but also the ordinary people, and especially the poets.

The latter, being the only educated people of the day and, consequently, the only voice of the peasant class, were always considered dangerous. They were forced to go on the run on many occasions when their compositions were declared seditious, particularly Art McCooey, Peadar Ó Doirnín, and the legendary poet-cum-Rapparee Séamas Mór Mac Murchú. In fact it was on one such occasion, as we shall hear shortly, that Art McCooey composed his most famous poem, ÚrChill An Chreagáin.

Art gives voice often in his poetry to this oppression of himself and his people under the new English Overlords, the Clann Bhullaigh, and the severe changes in their fortunes since the downfall of native rule, represented for Art, as we said before, by the O' Neills. This is his most common political theme and, in fact, his most frequent theme generally.

Art, however, deals often with more basic things, such as the main foods of the ordinary people, especially potatoes, porridge, milk, butter and buttermilk. There is no mention anywhere of beef. Drink, as we might imagine, is mentioned often, particularly whiskey, beer, and wine. The latter, however, is associated only with the houses of the upper classes and, perhaps significantly, with the house of the Parish Priest. The crop mentioned as being the most common, and perhaps the most important, was flax and the spinning of flax thread as being one of the most common jobs of the women.

In Art's case there is clear evidence that he found it difficult to hold down a job for any length of time, his two abiding interests being poetry and, I'm afraid, drink. This is illustrated by a well-documented story concerning him.

One springtime Art got work with a farmer named Jones at Layther Hill sliping manure from the farmyard to a field at the top of the hill. Art filled his load in the dunghill and set off. It was a beautiful spring morning with the birds singing all around him and Art soon got lost in the reverie of thought and of poetic composition. When he reached the top of the hill he turned around, forgetting to empty the load, and headed back down again. When he had taken the same load up and down three times Jones finally caught on and, with a string of curses, sent Art packing. It is no wonder that his life was one of virtual penury, as he makes clear in his poem ÚrChill An Chreagáin.

Many of Art's poems give an insight into his personal life and cast a clear light on some of the more turbulent periods of his passage through Creggan, incurring as he did the wrath of many people in authority, not just Johnston of the Fews.

Art's most celebrated row was undoubtedly the one with the local Parish Priest, the Rev Fr. Terence Quinn, which resulted in Art being banished from Creggan and forced to live at Howth, something which caused him a great deal of grief.

The origins of this row are many, but the seeds of the final bust up were undoubtedly sown in the scathing satire which Art wrote on the Priest's sister, Mary. It should be noted at this stage that the said Fr. Quinn had the reputation of looking with more favour on the well-to-do than on the lowly peasants and of being very harsh in the dues which he levied on his parishioners. This was first highlighted in a satire written by McCooey's contemporary, Peadar Ó Doirnín. Some years later the parishioners themselves had finally to have recourse to the Primate of the day, Archbishop Blake, concerning the matter. Because of this Art would have already been ill-disposed to the Rev. Quinn. The matter was finally brought to a head on an occasion when Art suffered a severe rebuff at the hands of the Priest's sister, Mary.

What happened was that Art had called to the Parochial House on business in his role as gardener. The Priest's sister was entertaining two important visitors, business men who were in to pay their dues. At that time dues were not paid in money but in kind, e.g. potatoes, yarn, cloth, butter etc. Mary showed the visitors into the parlour and served them up wine. When Art called at the front door Mary wouldn't let him in but hunted him around to the servants' quarters, where he was served up buttermilk in the back kitchen. Art, who was always so keenly aware of the honour once afforded to poets, took this as a terrible affront. He gave vent to his rage in a blistering satire on the Priest's sister. As it happened the lady in question had a squint in her eye and Art started in good vein in the title of the poem itself, Máire Chaoch – Blind Mary!

Below is a spirited translation of the piece done by Cardinal Tomás Ó Fiaich R.I.P., which catches the rakish, but biting, quality of the original:

BLIND MARY QUINN

"All the children around are in tatters for dress
And the people can't pay the funeral cess,
Yarn and cloth have run out and the seed has grown thin
And there's butter for no one but Blind Mary Quinn.

Any upstart brought up without a square meal,
From Legmoylin below to Clarebane of O' Neill,
If his linen is spun and his praties are in
Will be treated to wine by Blind Mary Quinn.

A handsome young fellow is not what would please her,
Who'd give her a kiss and maybe would squeeze her,
But the bloke with a present of spuds for the bin,
'Tis he'd drink the punch with Blind Mary Quinn.

McCooey the poet she reckoned unable
To drink with the gentry or sit at the table,
But in some nook or cranny perched up on his legs
He drained all the buttermilk down to the dregs.

If the heroes of Oriel were still in this land
They wouldn't allow his verse to be banned
Nor suffer the huxters to kick up a din,
Entertained in the Priest's house by Blind Mary Quinn.

'Tis my grief Father Felim is locked in the clay
For his like is not found in the parish today,
Every heart felt sore grief when his grave was closed in,
And none was rejoicing but Blind Mary Quinn.

> *Good luck and success every step that he'll take*
> *To our Bishop and Primate, the warm-hearted Blake,*
> *'Tis he will clean up the mess that we're in,*
> *And lessen the swagger of Blind Mary Quinn."*

Father Quinn was incensed by this satire and his ire was added to by the fact that his parishioners, in contrast, gave it a very warm reception and it soon became a local "hit". Many hold that it was because of this that Art was banished from the Parish of Creggan, but that is only part of the truth.

Art had met and fallen in love with a local girl, Mary Lamb, and they wished to get married. However, they were second cousins, a band of relationship inside which marriage was forbidden by Church law without a special dispensation from the Pope. This would normally have been a mere formality. The crunch was that such a dispensation could only be sought by the Parish Priest. Father Quinn, in a fit of pique because of Art's satire, refused to make the application. Art, in an equal fit of pique, defied the priest and went ahead and got married in the Protestant Church of Creggan, something completely unheard of at the time. This act according to ecclesiastical law, carried automatic excommunication, a penalty that Father Quinn imposed and Art was hunted from the Parish. It appears that the excommunication was performed in full formal fashion with "bell, book, and candle." In a later satire which Art wrote on a family called O' Callaghan who incurred his wrath he refers to it. This satire is entitled Bodaigh Na hEorna — The Churls of the Barley, and in one verse Art says:

> *"I'm a pauper, they say, a rascal, a stray*
> *And there's nothing but lies in my singing.*
> *If I don't disappear, the Parish will hear*
> *The bells for my interdict ringing."*

On his expulsion from the Parish Art went to Howth where he spent more than a year. However, he was extremely homesick and his mind was constantly on Creggan and also, as one might imagine, on the O' Neills. The nostalgia which he felt there is clearly visible in his compositions of that period, as in the following extract from one of his "Vision Poems", translated by Cardinal Tomás Ó Fiaich:

"By Howth's fair haven on the edge of Erin,
I lay in waiting beside the sea,
When a sweet-lipped maiden, to me a stranger,
Appeared like Venus or some strange Banshee,
Who there related how a hundred brave men
Rose from Creggan graveyard, by the tombs released,
And our own Uí Néill were once more in state there
And the Fews sustained them with gold and beast.

I moved adjacent as I was able
When her northern tale fell upon my ears
And I asked was Turlough, the son of Henry,
Restoring the greatness of bygone years,
Or had some foul traitor against our brave ones
Burnt down Dunreavey, nor left a tree,
Could my fair maid say with her information
Was young Eoghan O' Neill back across the sea?"

Art eventually enlisted the aid of Father Lawrence Taffe, the Parish Priest of Kilkerley, who intervened on his behalf and finally managed to get the excommunication lifted. He also arranged for the required dispensation which would allow Art to marry Mary Lamb according to the Catholic rite. To help "pave his way" Art wrote another poem on "Blind Mary", but this time in a completely different vein, an exquisite piece entitled Cúilfhionn Ní Choinne — Fair-haired Beauty of the Quinns. This is as far removed from the original Máire Chaoch as one can imagine, extolling as it does the beauty and the virtues of the said Mary to the skies! Poetically speaking, this is one of Art's most perfect pieces and is second only in repute to ÚrChill An Chreagáin. It is difficult to believe that it is about the same woman. My own translation below of one of the verses will suffice to illustrate the difference:

"Out along the way there's a fair young maid,
Her sweet voice gay, stepping o'er the road,
And all nature ceases to listen to her greetings
Captivated by her sweetness every day of the year.

Her white teeth flashing like bright ivy dancing,
Beneath the sun prancing, all along the way;
Her yellow hair blowing like dulcet honey flowing,
Her bright skin glowing — 'Tis my Mary dear!"

The piece seems to have served the required purpose. Art was allowed to return home and marry Mary Lamb in the Catholic Church, thus ending a very turbulent period of his life.

As we said, Art's best-known song is ÚrChill An Chreagáin - The Sweet Churchyard of Creggan, written while Art was on the run from Johnston of the Fews, and hiding in Creggan graveyard. This song was to become one of the most popular songs of Ulster as a whole, and almost the National Anthem of South East Ulster, right up to the end of the Gaelic Era. It is still one of the most frequently sung pieces in Gaelic circles throughout Ireland to this day.

It is virtually impossible to convey in English the beauty of this composition with its lilting cadence and internal agreement of vowel sounds in each line, culminating in the long o sound at the end of the line. The first and fourth foot in every line has a long vowel sound; the second and third foot has the same sound repeated, a short hard a; and the last foot, as we said, ends in the long o sound. If we look briefly at the first verse it will be clear what I mean:

In **Ú**irchill an Chreag**á**in a chad**ai**l mé ar**é**ir faoi bhr**ó**n
Is le h**é**ir**í** na maidne th**á**inig **a**innir fá mo dh**é**in le p**ó**ig;
Bhí gr**í**os-ghrua gh**a**rtha aici 'gus lainnir ina c**é**ibh mar **ó**r
's gurb é **í**ocshl**á**inte an d**o**mhain bheith ag **a**mharc ar an r**i**oghain
óig.

In the above I have highlighted the stressed vowel sounds in each line. If these are said on their own, with the full sound value given to each, the effect is something very close to music. The long o sound, especially, at the end of the line is extremely effective. This, maintained the whole way down through the poem, has the effect of turning what is a "Vision Poem" into a lament, which in many ways is what this piece really is. In it Art uses the

Heavenly Maiden very skilfully to give voice to all his own trials, sufferings, and deprivations, which personal decorum would not allow himself to say.

A direct imitation of the metrical format of this poem in English will nearly always produce a "jingle" effect, which is completely absent in the original Irish. The reason is that English does not have the long and short system vowel sounds which exists in Irish and which would allow such a format to be feasible.

There are only two ways to attempt a translation. The first is to depart completely from the Irish format and attempt to convey the quality of the original in the beauty of the language employed in English, as Dr. Sigerson did in his well-known translation, or to attempt to keep closer to the Irish by employing at least some of the metrical devices used there. It was the latter approach which I followed in the translation below. I very quickly dismissed the possibility of imitating the long vowel sounds in the first and fourth foot of every line, as I knew it simply could not be achieved in English. Instead I set myself the task of keeping the "Comhfhuaim" – Repeated Stressed Sound, in the middle of each line, together with the long o at the end. Even with that I found it impossible to base the Comhfhuaim on the hard a vowel sound, as McCooey does throughout. I include the translation here in the hope that it may motivate someone down the line to attempt to take it further with more success.

The Sweet Churchyard Of Creggan

'Midst Creggan's dead numbered I slumbered last night in deep woe
And with the morning's bright dawning there approached me a maid on tiptoe.
Her countenance was fair and her hair had the sheen of pure gold
And a cure for all ills was the thrill her sweet form to behold.

"Oh, most generous of men do not spend your days in such throes
But cease from your worries and hurry with me o'er the road
To the land of the free we both knew where sweet honey flows,
Where in hallways of leisure sweet pleasure awaits us as of old."

166

"For no wealth of this land your fair hand would I spurn now, or more,
Save for those friends I'd offend should I part from these shores,
And still more my wife whom I enticed with my promises galore,
Should I part from her now sure I know her heart would be sore

"No boon to you now do I vow are those same friends of yours
When barren and bare is your share of this world's store.
Much better in lioses my kisses and charms to explore
Than this land to be mocking and scoffing at your every poem."

"Oh, most beautiful maiden, are you Helen of Troy's overthrow,
Or of the nine fair graces of Parnassus of beauty untold,
Or from what land in this world do you hail, oh star of pure gold,
That one such as me should e'er be your first choice o'er the road.?"

"Not to this land of the Boyne would I deign my allegiance to owe
But to the bright fairy world where I was culled from the heart of
Gráinne Óg.
Where poets assemble I am present to inspire their pure odes,
At night-time in Tara and tomorrow on the plain of Tyrone.

"Alas for this land that they've gone, those Gaels of Tyrone!
And these heirs of the Fews whom we view beneath this dark stone.
No voices they'll raise now in praise of Erin's sweet songs,
Nor these descendants of Frasach with largess embellish their poets!"

Since Aughrim's dark plunder and the sunder of Boyne's bloody shore
Where the scions of Banba were mangled in blood and foul gore
Much better by far to declare with me to my world
Than bear through your heart the sharp darts of John Bull evermore.

"Fair maid of the Heavens, if it is destined that with you I must go,
Come pledge to me now this one vow ere my feet hit the road,--
Should I die 'round the Shannon, in Manannan, or on Egypt's wide
shore,
'Midst the fair Gaels of Creggan may I rest in true peace for evermore."

McCooey's long-held dream that the O' Neills would somehow rise again was finally shattered in 1769 with the sudden and tragic death at the age of twenty six of the young man in whom all his hopes were enshrined, Art Óg Ó Néill, the son of Daniel. It is only in his final grand lament on the death of Art Óg that McCooey finally concedes the shattering of his dream. In this, his most poignant poem, which runs to two hundred and sixty lines and which is a celebration of all the long line of the O' Neills from the earliest times, Art faces the stark reality of his life. He stands now alone, with not only his great champions gone but also the great poets of the era, men such as Randal Dall Mac Dónaill, Pádraig Mac A' Liondáin, and Séamas Dall Mac Cuarta. He is virtually a voice in the wilderness. He puts the following lines into the mouth of the Heavenly Maiden through whom most of the lament is uttered:

I am the headless corpse of the Fews
Once renowned beneath Henry's rule,
By the Bards of old dubbed land of the O' Neills,
The fragrant garden of the tribe of the Gael
Once roamed by Earls and Princes bold
In my castle tall by Dunreavey wood.

Since Milesius' sons came o'er the sea
From the land of Spain, tall and fair,
No hour have I spent without the hero's tread
Of a true Gael's foot here by my side,
Never until now 'till the sod has claimed
Art Óg Ó Néill, the last warrior Gael.

Well may they weep those mountainsides
From Wexford Head to Moy Leana's brow,
From Derry of the ships to Howth's fair waves,
From Patrick's Fort to the Rath of Maeve
O'er the death of the prince due Erin's crown
If this land had remained to O' Neill the Proud.

And if there still lived the Bards of old,
Mc Court himself would have raised your keen
And Mac Alinden too would thee endow
And Mac Dónaill Dall would wreath your brow.
But since none remain but I alone
My lament I raise on the winds forlorn.

The exact number of McCooey's compositions is not known. Those that have come down to us owe their survival to the Trojan work of two men, first of all Art Bennett from Ballykeel, beside Mullaghbawn, and later Henry Morris from Monaghan. The latter published the works that had been collected in 1926.

Art Bennett was born just twenty years after the death of Art McCooey, in the year 1793. He was a stonemason by trade, but he was also a Gaelic speaker, a scribe, and a poet in his own right. He spent nearly all his spare time travelling around the South Armagh area, and further afield, collecting the songs and poems of McCooey from the lips of the last generation of native speakers. He was assisted in this by the Mc Adam family from Belfast who acted as his patrons, supplying him with writing material, ink, and occasional modest sums of money. According to Art's letters the latter was much too occasional and very frequently too modest. He often complains of lack of materials and of sufficient money to allow him to continue his work.

Art Bennett was very aware of the importance of the work he was doing and also of its urgency and was frequently frustrated by his slow progress and missed opportunities. On a number of occasions he laments to the Mc Adam family that when he finally managed to get to a house where he was told an old person lived who knew a song of McCooey's he found the person in question had died and that the younger generation had had no interest not only in learning the song but even in learning the language itself, all of them being English speaking.

Art was very aware that he was no more than scratching the surface of McCooey's output. This was brought home to him forcefully on an occasion which is one of the most widely documented tales in oral tradition concerning him at this time.

In comparatively recent years new research has proved quite conclusively that by the middle of the eighteenth century, McCooey's period, poets had begun to keep personal manuscripts of their poems, something that had never been done in Ireland before. This gives immediate credence to the above-mentioned, long-held tale.

It would appear that on one occasion when Art was returning home from work he called into a shop in Mounthill owned by a man called Tom Lamb. The woman of the house was behind the counter parcelling up a loaf for a young lad. Art noticed that there seemed to be something strange about the paper which she was using. He asked her where she had got it. She replied, "When we took over this house there was a full trunk of this stuff up in the attic. Lately paper has been very scarce and, do you know, it fits lovely around a loaf!" Art asked her would she mind if he took a look at it. She said that she wouldn't but that there were only a couple of sheets left. When Art examined it he found that it was, as he thought, the manuscripts of Art McCooey's poetry, parcelled up around loaves and scattered to the four winds!

This is only one of many stories that can be told concerning the ravages that time has wrought on all of these poets, the leading figures of the last great Gaelic literary age in Ireland. In my youth not only was their work not known, but their very names had passed from memory.

In 1969 a committee was set up consisting of people from South Armagh and North Louth, called Éigse Oirialla, which set itself the task of trying to undo some of this injustice. Major research was done on each poet in turn, with a book published containing his poetic output and also an account of his life and times. A major weekend celebration was held in his honour at which the book was launched, followed by lectures, entertainment, a school of poetry, trips around the poet's area, and the unveiling of a memorial in his honour at the site of his burial. The first Poet to be so honoured was Peadar ó Doirnín, followed by Séamas Dall Mac Cuarta and Cathal Buí Mac Giolla Gunna. In 1973 it came the turn of Art McCooey.

Unlike in the case of some of the other poets, a fair number of facts were already known concerning Art McCooey, especially the date of his death.

Cardinal Tomás Ó Fiaich took on the task of doing the research on Art's life and work, a task which he assumed with relish as he was a fellow countryman of McCooey's.

Because of the unique connection between Art and the O' Neills, a fact that caused him to be referred to often in Irish as File Na Niallach, the Poet of the O' Neills, the committee felt that recognition should be given to this fact somewhere in Art's celebration. It had long been held in oral tradition that the O' Neills, who had built Creggan Church around the year 1480, had had an underground burial vault somewhere in the graveyard. The committee felt that this would be an excellent opportunity for them to meet their objective, if the location of the vault could be found. After exhaustive enquiries, however, it had to be accepted that the location of such a vault was not known in living memory. There was a great deal of debate on the committee concerning this matter, some holding that the vault was merely a myth, part of the romance of the legend surrounding McCooey, and others stoutly declaring that oral tradition is seldom wrong. According to this tradition it was actually in the vault that McCooey was hiding when he composed ÚrChill An Chreagáin. However, since no vault could be discovered a different strategy had to be found.

Someone on the committee put forward the idea of trying to find a family on the Continent, to which the O' Neills had been banished by Cromwell, in direct line of descent from the royal O' Neills of South Armagh, and to invite a representative to participate in the celebration of their champion poet.

Tomás Ó Fiaich who had great skill in these matters undertook the quest.

He eventually discovered just such a family, in Seville in Spain. They were, in fact, members of the Spanish aristocracy, and their leader, Don Carlos, was a count. They were descended from a young man, Red Henry, who was the grandson of the last leader of the Royal O' Neills in Connacht, a man called Henry. He left Creggan shortly after his people were banished from Ireland. He established a new dynasty in Spain which played a very distinguished role in Spanish military history, gaining much greater distinction than the Creggan O' Neills ever had in Ireland. Don Carlos held a number of titles, Count Don Carlos Ó Néill, Condé De Lá Norté and Fifth Marquis De Lá Granja.

This family knew absolutely nothing about their illustrious Irish ancestry, and when Cardinal Ó Fiaich presented them with their family tree they were both flabbergasted and delighted. They declared immediately that they wished to be part of the celebration and that the whole family would come to Creggan, the memorial to be unveiled by Don Carlos' daughter, countess Conchita Ó Néill — It is interesting to note that, unlike in Ireland, the original Gaelic form of the family name had never changed on the continent.

This news was greeted with great excitement by the committee but also with some little anxiety as it added to the urgency of the preparations required. One thing that needed immediate attention was the graveyard, which was in nothing like the neat condition in which it is today. A local man, Jem Murphy, who took great delight in the fact that he was a direct descendant of the famous outlaw and poet, Séamas Mór Mc Murphy, gathered a group of local men and started into clearing the place up. During the course of their work they had to bring in a tractor to remove rubble. One evening the tractor got bogged down in soft earth up behind the Church. When they pulled it out they discovered that there seemed to be a hole underneath the spot where the wheel had sunk. When they removed the topsoil they found a large, thick slate which the wheel had broken. When they removed the slate they found that they were looking at the entrance to the O' Neill underground burial vault!

When some local men, together with Cardinal Tomás Ó Fiaich, went down into the vault they discovered a large number of bones, laid out in neat rows. They counted eighty complete skulls, together with fragments of approximately twenty more, virtually all the line of the great O' Neills from the time that they arrived in South Armagh.

The discovery of the vault in this manner was a remarkable, if not exceedingly strange, coincidence. When I heard the news I felt the hair rising on the back of my neck. It was as if the event was too farfetched for reality. If the tractor wheel had gone a foot either way the existence of the vault would still be part only of folklore. Since its discovery was directly linked with the preparations for the honouring of the celebrated O' Neill poet it was as if McCooey was still championing the cause of his legendry heroes even from the grave.

It was later discovered that the vault had been closed around the year 1845 by the Rector of the period, Rev. Atkinson. It appears that one of the last of the O' Neills to be interred there was a priest, Fr. Felim O' Neill, most likely the man to whom Art refers in his satire Blind Mary.

Apparently he was a very saintly man and held in very high esteem by the local people. As a consequence they were making frequent visits to his grave, much to the annoyance of the Rev. Atkinson.

The reason why the location of the vault had been lost turned out to be quite simple. It was exactly where you would have expected it to be, provided you were aware of one thing. The original Church built by the O' Neills came into the occupancy of the Church of Ireland after the Reformation, and its layout was changed, the cruciform shape being altered. Where the vault is situated is the point to which the main aisle of the original Church would have reached. The O' Neill vault was, in fact, located beneath the main altar, as one would expect for a family of such distinction. When you entered the vault on its discovery the outline of the passageway, then filled with stones, which once led up into the Church was clearly visible.

The discovery of the O' Neill vault gave added significance to parts of McCooey's poem, ÚrChill An Chreagáin. If we look, for example, at the line:

"Oidhríbh an Fheadha gan seaghas faoi léig dár gcomhair — The Heirs of the Fews sadly before me beneath this flagstone", it would appear that it was, indeed, in the vault that McCooey was when he composed it.

As we said, Art McCooey died in 1773. It was always held that he was born in the year 1715, a date that would have given him a fairly reasonable lifespan. However, during the course of his research Cardinal Tomás Ó

Fiaich discovered that that date was wrong and that he could not have been born before the year 1738, a fact that gave an added poignancy to his life. It meant that he died a very young man, in his thirty sixth year. It is amazing that in such a short lifetime, dogged by hardship and poverty, not to mention controversy, he should have achieved so much. It is a sad fact that he left much more wealth behind him than he ever enjoyed in his own life. If you stand at the memorial tombstone raised by Éigse Oirialla in his memory, there is only one great wish of his life that you can know for certain was ever fulfilled, the one expressed in the last two lines of his celebrated song, composed here in this graveyard:

Should I die 'round the Shannon, in Manannan, or on Egypt's wide shore, 'Midst the fair Gaels of Creggan may I rest in true peace for evermore."

Dr. Patrick Donnelly

(The Bard of Armagh)

Patrick Donnelly was born in the year 1649 in the townland of Gortalowry, in the parish of Desertcreat in Co. Tyrone. He was descended from one of the celebrated Gaelic Clans of the previous era, the Clann Uí Dhonnghaile, who by the time of Bishop Donnelly's great grandfather, Donall Gruama Ó Donnghaile, in the late 16th century, were closely linked to the ruling dynasty of the O' Neills with whom they claimed kinship.

Patrick Donnelly lived through one of the most turbulent periods in Ireland's history, the second half of the 17th century and the beginning of the 18th, a period that was to witness the final total eclipse of these great Gaelic Clans who had formed the central core of Irish society for centuries, and who had been the pillars of the Catholic Church. They were replaced by a new ascendancy who were completely out of sympathy with both native Irish interests and with Catholicism. Through various stages of persecutions, banishments, and draconian laws the Catholic Church was brought to its knees. For a number of years the only person who stood between its survival and the ultimate fulfilment of Cromwell's stated wish to see a total end to Catholicism in Ireland was the man whom we are dealing with here, Dr. Patrick Donnelly, Bishop of Dromore, and Bard of Armagh.

In the decade prior to Patrick Donnelly's birth things had begun to look up for both the Irish society and the Catholic Church. After the rising of 1641, once more spear-headed by the O'Neills, and the setting up of the Catholic parliament, the Confederation of Kilkenny, the Church began to take its first tentative steps on the long road back from the ravishes of the Elizabethan era, followed by the first stage of the plantations and the accompanying severe anti-catholic laws put into operation under James I.

This rising was different to the first rising of the Earls in 1595, which saw their almost total annihilation at Kinsale, in that it crossed the cultural demarcation line in Ireland, embracing both the native Gaels and the landed catholic aristocracy of the Pale, that coastal strip from Dundalk down to Dublin first planted by the Anglo-Normans, and embracing Co. Meath the homeland of the Plunkett family.

This rising was essentially an anti-reformation struggle where both sides were united in the common cause of their religion, to the backdrop of a major threat coming from England where a predominantly protestant parliament was trying to wrest power from the king. With the arrival from Spain of Hugh O' Neill's nephew, Owen Roe O' Neill, to take charge of the Irish forces the native catholic armies were in the ascendancy. Catholic churches were opened once more, schools set up, priests ordained and Bishops consecrated. For a time a better future was being presaged for the Catholic Church than had been its recent bitter past. All this was to change utterly in the very year that Patrick Donnelly was born, in 1649, with the arrival of Cromwell in Ireland.

It would be difficult to overstate the devastating effect of the decade of Cromwellian occupation on the society of Ireland and on the Catholic Church. The second purge of the Earls took place which saw the survivors of the first plantation banished from the country, or, like the O' Neill dynasty of South Armagh, sent to the bog lands of Connacht. This was paralleled by an anti-catholic backlash unseen in the previous history of Ireland, as if Catholicism itself were on trial for its life for daring to raise its head above the parapet and challenge the perceived authority in the land. To be a catholic now was to be in a position of danger and to be a cleric was to be a member of the hunted class.

The Donnellys had risen with the O'Neills in the first rising of 1595 in the time of Patrick's great grandfather, Donall Gruama, and again in 1641 in the person of Bishop Donnelly's own father, Patrick Donnelly. After the first rising the Donnellys had lost all their lands and were reduced to the status of small tenant farmers on the former great Gaelic estates. In 1610 Donall Gruama's son Shane, Bishop Donnelly's grandfather, was granted the tenancy of 60 acres of land, including a number of acres of shrub land and five acres of bog in the Desertcreat area. This would have given a secure, though modest, income to the family during the early years of Bishop Donnelly's childhood. In the Cromwellian confiscations, however, this land also was lost and the family were cast to the wayside, like so many other Gaelic families of the time. These confiscations came into force in 1659 when the young Patrick was just turned ten years of age, and for him life would never be the same again. Whatever education he would receive from now on would have to be gained, like so many other things in his later life, in secret, depending as he was on the resources available to him in the hedge schools. Part of his survival would depend on his skills as a musician, an art handed down to him through many generations of his Gaelic ancestry where music, as in the case of all the great Gaelic Clans, was an integral part of Clan lifestyle. It is not at all surprising that it should be the disguise of a wandering minstrel that he would adopt later in life when Bishop of Dromore, hiding out in the small town land of Doctor's Quarters.

During the tribulations of the Cromwellian era the man who was to be Patrick Donnelly's later friend and mentor, Oliver Plunkett, was in Rome. He was ordained in 1654 when the atrocities were at their highest and shortly afterwards his family too were left landless, his father losing all his ancestral estates, some 680 acres, in Co. Meath.

In 1669, the year before Oliver Plunkett arrived in Ireland as Primate, the ravishes of the Cromwellian period were all too evident in his native land. All the four Archiepiscopal Seas of Armagh, Dublin, Tuam and Cashel were without occupants. Neither was there a Bishop anywhere in Ulster. In fact the only working Bishop in the whole of Ireland was his own kinsman, Patrick Plunkett, who was then Bishop of Ardagh. All Catholic Churches were either closed or occupied by other denominations. There was no education of any kind officially on offer for the catholic youth of the country, something which appalled the new Primate even more than many of the other problems that he had to face on his arrival. Its effect could be seen amongst the younger priests who had been ordained in the previous decade, mostly by the lone Bishop Patrick Plunkett. Their education was at best rudimentary and their ecclesiastical training was virtually nil. This was a problem which he felt had to be addressed immediately. He very quickly came to the conclusion that he had no other option but to set up schools himself.

In July 1670, just some four months after his arrival in Ireland, Oliver Plunkett in a letter to Rome stated that he had already built "from the foundations a commodious (mass)house and two schools." There were already150 students attending the schools and 25 ecclesiastics. In the following year the number of priests had risen to 56. As Cardinal Ó Fiaich R.I.P. says in his book on the life of Oliver Plunkett, it is quite likely that with few exceptions all the priests of the Armagh Diocese were routed through these schools for retraining in the next couple of years.

Among the students attracted to these schools, situated in Ballybarrak outside Dundalk, was Patrick Donnelly from Desertcreat, then in his twenty first year. Another student from this area who was later to become a very close friend of his was John McParland. This man completed his education in the schools in Ballybarrak just before Oliver Plunkett moved them to Drogheda in the year 1672. He was ordained in the same year in Ballybarrak and took up residence in Lathbirget where he was to remain for the rest of his life. He was Parish Priest of Upper Killeavy during the time that Patrick Donnelly was Bishop of Dromore and living here in Doctor's Quarters, less than a mile from Fr. McParland's house.

In the following year, 1673, Patrick Donnelly was ordained by Oliver Plunkett in Ballybarrak, a member of the last group of priests to be ordained there by the Primate. He was appointed curate in Armagh city (the Parish of Armagh), a position that he was to hold for the next six years.

It is very likely that he lived in Armagh city or its environs during that period.

Only a matter of months after the ordination of Patrick Donnelly things took a dramatic turn for the worse for the Catholic Church in Ireland. The protestant parliament in England, still in a very strong position, finally forced its will on the restoration king, Charles 11, and issued a decree dissolving all Church property. Oliver Plunkett's schools in Drogheda were razed to the ground and a short time later, on the 18th January 1674, Oliver Plunkett and his close friend John Brennan, Bishop of Cashel, were forced to flee and seek shelter in the South Armagh hills, coming first to this area of Slieve Gullion. This flight is well documented by Oliver Plunkett himself in a letter written by him to the Internuncio in Rome on 27th January 1674 from his first hideout, the house of a "reduced gentleman who had nothing to lose" and who gave them shelter as they fled during a violent snowstorm in that bitter winter of 1673/74, fearing for their lives due to the great depth of snow in the valleys.

The location of this house is traditionally given as the valley of Mullaghbawn, where exactly we do not know. It is clear, however, that this valley in the lee of Slieve Gullion was frequented often by the Primate during the next five years on the many occasions that he had to hide out, as was, indeed, Slieve Gullion mountain itself.

There is a very strong oral tradition linking Oliver Plunkett with the small house that stands in Doctor's Quarters on the site of what is now known as Sally Humphreys house, the place where Patrick Donnelly was to spend the last twenty odd years of his life while Bishop of Dromore. This link is quite significant and not easily ignored.

The well below the house which supplied water to the various families occupying this house down through the generations, including in the time of Patrick Donnelly, is to this day known as Oliver Plunkett's well. Also, the mass rock in the secluded dell up behind the house where many generations of priests celebrated mass, including most likely Bishop Donnelly himself when he first arrived here, and later during the crisis caused by the Oath of Abjuration in 1710, has always been referred to in an unbroken line of tradition in the Murphy family, on whose property it stands, as Oliver Plunkett's mass rock. In addition, until recent years, another mass rock stood just across the road from there on James McParland's land, also in Doctor's Quarters. It was cherished in the memory of that family, and assiduously cared for, as a rock on which Oliver Plunkett had said mass.

This evidence, particularly the evidence of the well, would suggest very strongly that this house was one of the "cabins" referred to in "the valley of Mullaghbawn" where the Primate hid out on one or more occasions during the years 1674 and 1679 when he was forced to go on the run. There is, indeed, a possibility that it may in fact be the actual house referred to by the Primate in that famous letter of 27th January 1674. It is equally very likely that his young curate, Patrick Donnelly, with whom he had a close relationship, was familiar with this and other hideouts used by the Primate, explaining why he himself immediately headed for this area, and this house, in later years when he too had to seek shelter, knowing that he would be granted a safe haven here.

During the early years of his Primacy Oliver Plunkett was constantly petitioning Rome to allow him to send five or six of his best students to the College of Propaganda Fide for further education. He argued that, whereas he could prepare students adequately for the priesthood in his Irish schools, he could not supply the level of education necessary to equip them for the positions that so urgently needed to be filled in the upper hierarchy of the Church, particularly the positions of Vicar General and Bishop. For this he felt they would need a doctorate, something that they could only acquire by going abroad. — "It is necessary that there be here some men with doctorates who can account for the things that they believe." Since the small number of places on offer for Irish students in Rome at that time were reserved almost exclusively for students from Munster, he eventually turned his attention to other centres of learning, especially the college of Louvain and the Irish college in Paris.

This explains why in the year 1679 we see the young curate Patrick Donnelly heading off under the mentorship of the Primate to study for a

Doctor's degree at the Collège des Lombards on the left bank of the Seine which had been founded by exiled Irish priests during the Elizabethan era.

Shortly after Patrick Donnelly's departure Oliver Plunkett was arrested, 5th December 1679 and imprisoned. During the course of his later trials and final execution, 1st July 1681, there is no record of Patrick Donnelly being in Ireland. In records still extant for the year 1681 of bursaries granted to students in the Collège des Lombards there appears the name of Patrick Donnelly and, very interestingly, the name of his younger brother, Terence Donnelly, who was later to be appointed Bishop of Derry.

Patrick Donnelly remained at the Collège des Lombards for six years in all and adequately fulfilled the promise that his mentor had seen in him, graduating with a joint doctorate in both Civil Law and Church, or Canon, Law.

On his return to Ireland in 1685 he was appointed Parish Priest of Keady, a position he was to hold for a number of years. There is a possibility that he may have spent a time at first as Parish Priest of Louth. This, however, is not entirely certain. In the early 1690's he was elevated to the position of Vicar General of the Archdiocese of Armagh and Vice-Primate, filling in for the then Archbishop and Primate Dominic Maguire who, for reasons best known to himself, remained throughout the duration of his office in voluntary exile in Paris, at the royal Court of Saint Germain, the residence of the deposed Stewart King, James 11. Some years later, around the mid-1690's, he was moved to occupy the same positions in the diocese of Dromore, which still was without a Bishop. Finally in the year 1697 he was appointed Bishop of Dromore. In the documents pertaining to his appointment it states that since there were no churches or mass houses anywhere in the diocese of Dromore mass would have to be celebrated in parishioners' houses, or in the open.

The appointment of Patrick Donnelly as Bishop of Dromore could scarcely have fallen at a more inauspicious time, virtually coinciding, as it did, with one of the more draconian of the Penal Law Acts and one whose very name gave clear indications of its intent, the Suppression of Popery Act. This act, amongst many other provisions, banned all Bishops permanently from the country. Immediately on his appointment, therefore, as Bishop of Dromore Patrick Donnelly was officially an outlaw. Also, as a result of the panic spread throughout the country by this act, Patrick Donnelly was one of only two Bishops now left in the whole of Ireland, the other being the aged and infirm Bishop of Cashel, John Brennan, who was permanently confined to bed and unable to carry our any functions, either as Bishop or priest, including celebrating mass. Bishop Donnelly was, therefore, on his appointment, the only active Bishop in the whole of Ireland in the year 1697, a situation that was to remain unchanged for the next ten years, until he himself consecrated the next Bishops in the year 1707.

The new Bishop had no alternative but to go into hiding. He followed the footsteps of his illustrious friend and mentor, Oliver Plunkett, and headed for the security of the South Armagh hills, returning one feels to a hideout here in Doctor's Quarters already well known to him.

Doctor Donnelly spent the next twenty two years of his life, up until his death, here. Throughout the main part of the year he worked as an ordinary peasant farmer tilling the fields around his cabin, undistinguishable from the rest of the community. During the summer months he took to the roads in his celebrated disguise of a wandering minstrel, under the alias Felim Brady, and did an annual Episcopal tour of the whole diocese of Dromore, returning normally in September.

In the year 1704 the Suppression of Popery Act was taken a stage further, with the passing of the Act of Registration. This act required all catholic priests to sign an official register, giving their names, status in the Church, and permanent place of residence. They would be allowed to remain in their then abode but would not be allowed to have curates or to move outside their county. This had to be guaranteed by two bondsmen depositing sureties of £50 each, quite an enormous sum in those days. Those who did not sign the register would be, if later caught, subject to imprisonment. After much reflection the majority of priests in the Archdiocese of Armagh signed this register, as it gave them some form of security against arrest. Fr. John McParland appears on this register, his status given as Parish Priest of Upper Killeavy, and his place of residence as Lathbirget. His two bondsmen were Abraham Booth of Carrickasticken and Daniel Callaghan of Lislea.

The above concession did not apply to Bishops, who were still permanently banned from the country, thus ensuring that no further ordinations could be made. This left Bishop Donnelly in a quandary as he was the only person in reality to whom this applied. Being an expert on the workings of the civil law, and using the leeway available to him in canon law, Patrick Donnelly signed the register in Newry, giving his status as Parish priest of that area of the Newry parish which fell inside Armagh, and giving his place of residence as "Corrinallagh", the townland now known as Carricknagallia, of which the present small townland of Doctor's Quarters then formed part.

This subterfuge worked, but only for a short time. Two years later, in 1706 he was betrayed by a former priest, one John Duffy, who gave evidence under oath that Patrick Donnelly was actually a Bishop and that he had personally witnessed him ordaining priests and wearing the Bishop's mitre. He stated that he was residing in the house of Fr. John McParland.

Word was sent to Captain Walter Dawson in Armagh and he sent a representative, "one I could depend on", to investigate the matter. On the 9th September 1706 the house of Fr. John McParland in Lathbirget was raided. Word was sent back to Captain Dawson that no evidence had been found of a Patrick Donnelly living, or ever having lived, in the house of John McParland. Captain Dawson, however, reported to the authorities that his representative had found during the course of his investigation that there was a man by that name living "within a short mile" from Fr. McParland's house and that if this were the man in question he could soon have him apprehended. Receiving word to proceed, he himself, together with a sergeant and twelve men visited the area on the 14th September 1706 and raided the house of Bishop Donnelly in Doctor's Quarters. They apprehended Bishop Donnelly who had just returned from his annual Episcopal tour of his Diocese and brought him to Dundalk jail. A few days later he was transferred to prison in Dublin.

In the following months strenuous efforts were made to find witnesses to corroborate the evidence of John Duffy. But, despite all offers of bribes and threats of force, no one could be found to come forward to support John Duffy's claims, something which is a great testament to the esteem and affection in which Doctor Donnelly was held.

During the course of his imprisonment in Dublin the Bishop of Cashel died, thus leaving Patrick Donnelly literally and physically the only Bishop in the whole of Ireland.

Since there was no evidence forthcoming to corroborate Duffy's claims Patrick Donnelly was acquitted of all charges and released on the 13th May 1707.

With poetic irony Bishop Donnelly remained long enough in Dublin to consecrate three Bishops before returning home:-

Thaddeus O'Rourke, Bishop of Killala.
Edmund Byrne, Archbishop of Dublin.
Hugh McMahon, Bishop of Clogher.

The last crisis in the Catholic Church to confront Patrick Donnelly in his lifetime was the infamous period of the Oath of Abjuration. In the year 1709 an act was passed requiring all priests to take an oath of allegiance to the British Crown, in the person of Queen Ann, and renounce all support for the deposed Stuart line. To take such an oath was completely against the conscience of virtually all Irish clergy, as it was in the case of Patrick Donnelly. Not only was it opposed to official Vatican policy but it would be seen as an endorsement by the Irish clergy of all the anti-catholic laws passed in the name of the Crown, by which they would now be bound by the spirit of the oath. This they could not do. The final day for the swearing of the oath was given as 25thMarch 1710, a date referred to as "the fatal day". All priests who had not taken the oath by that day were to be hunted down and would be subject to the severest penalties. Substantial rewards were offered to anyone informing on such a priest.

In addition, the act provided that from that day forth anyone over the age of 16 could be forced to give evidence under oath of when and where he had last attended mass and who the celebrant had been.

This put priests in a very perilous position as their names and abodes were already known to the authorities from the registration of 1704, including Bishop Donnelly. It was no longer safe for any of them to celebrate mass in their normal places. Neither was it safe to say mass in public view of their parishioners, lest any of them would be forced to divulge under oath secrets which would be totally against their conscience.

For a period of time priests had to resort to other practices. It became common for mass to be celebrated in private houses with the congregation outside in the yard where they could hear mass through the open window but not see the celebrant. Alternatively mass was often celebrated at mass rocks with the parishioners stationed at a distance, or in a position, from which the celebrant could not be seen.

It is well known that Patrick Donnelly had a small mass house, close to his dwelling. Oral tradition indicates that it was in the area behind his house in the vicinity of the well. It is most likely that during this period he would have had to abandon this place for a time and say mass elsewhere. The obvious place would have been the mass rock used by his predecessor Oliver Plunkett in the secluded hollow to the north of his house. This place was ideally situated, being completely out of view from the main road, which at that time ran behind Doctor Donnelly's dwelling from Mullaghbawn, down the present laneway and across the valley towards Ballard.

In this regard there is an interesting, and significant, feature associated with the mass rock in question. During the childhood of the Murphy family, James Stephen and Lilly, whose house is adjacent to this mass rock, there was a dry trench, approximately six feet wide and quite deep, running behind the ditch which forms the perimeter of the mass rock site. Their mother, R.I.P., always referred to this trench, the outline of which is still visible, as "the hiding place". Given its open nature and its length it would not appear to have been the hiding place for a priest but rather for a group of people. It would have been an ideal position for parishioners to place themselves when mass was being celebrated at the nearby mass rock. They would be close enough to hear the mass but the celebrant would be completely obscured from their view. If this is the case there is little doubt that the celebrant during those troubled years would have been Bishop Donnelly.

Doctor Patrick Donnelly died sometime in the year 1719, not 1716 as has been generally accepted in most publications. The last letter written by him to the Irish College in Paris, thanking the Paris clergy for an annual stipend granted to him to assist with his upkeep, is dated clearly in the body of the letter as May 1719. This letter was lodged in the Stipendiary's office, close to the college, on 10th June 1719.

In an oral tradition well attested to, both in this area and the Desertcreat area of Tyrone, the enormous esteem in which Patrick Donnelly was held is shown by the fact that the parishioners carried his body by night from Doctors Quarters, each parish group handing him on to the next, the whole way back to his native parish of Desertcreat where his body now rests. His memory was later to be enshrined in the song The Bard of Armagh, still popular to the present day.

In the following year, 27th March 1720, Patrick Donnelly's brother, Terence Donnelly, was appointed Bishop of Derry, the first Bishop to be appointed there for 119 years, since the assassination of the last Bishop in 1601.

There is an oral tradition in parts of South Armagh which holds that Terence Donnelly was actually consecrated Bishop of Derry in the small chapel, or mass house, of his brother Patrick Donnelly in Doctor's Quarters. When I first heard this some years ago I was at first surprised. On reflection, knowing how close these men had been, it struck me that there was a distinct possibility that this could be true. It would be quite likely that Terence Donnelly knew this spot well and would have visited it, perhaps on many occasions, during the long tenure by his brother Patrick, especially during the latter years of his life. What more likely place could have been chosen, either by choice or necessity, than the place where his brother had laboured for twenty two years as Bishop of Dromore.

In relatively recent times documents assembled in Rome by Fr. Cathaldus Giblin pertaining to Irish matters, which provide considerable information on the last years of Doctor Donnelly's life, verify this oral tradition. In these documents it states that the consecration of Terence Donnelly as Bishop of

Derry took place "in the little chapel situated in the hiding place of the most illustrious Patrick, Bishop of Dromore."

And, so, the baton was handed on to another member of the illustrious Donnelly Clan of Tyrone, as it was to continue to be for the rest of the 18th century, a century in which the Church history of the Donaghmore area is dominated by the Donnelly name.

Patrick Donnelly had managed during one of the worst periods in Ireland's history to spend in all 46 years of his life as an ecclesiastic, moving through all the ranks of the Church from curate to Vice-Primate and Bishop, and still managed to die in his bed of old age. A remarkable achievement by a remarkable man whose importance in the history of the Catholic Church in Ireland is of great significance.

> *Down history's tortured path he walked*
> *Through lanes of mountain stone,*
> *Where moss now covers rocks once bared*
> *To quick of flesh and bone.*
>
> *And in these peasant fields he wrought,*
> *His spade God's spoken word*
> *Dug deep in soil of love and pain*
> *Where seeds of faith were sown.*
>
> *These hillsides were his pillared Church,*
> *These lanes his aisle and nave,*
> *His life both word and naked deed,*
> *His faith this altar laid.*

I am indebted to Seanchas Ard Mhaca for information concerning the life of Patrick Donelly.

UNDUG RIGS (collection of poems):

GOLDEN HILLSIDES

Flowers grow in whispers
Where Savants used to roam.
They speak in gentle mystery
Of what man will never know.
His is but to own.

I see them in the hillsides
And the meadows as I go.
They are our hidden gold.

Faith climbs in these hillsides
From the Churchyards
Where it's shrined,
Striving ever upwards
Towards the hands of God.

He raises it a chalice
To the sufferings of the past,
Red wine in gold of hillsides
Our offering and our Mass.

PEAKED

We are Slieve Gullion's Point,
Imminent to West and East,
Peaked on edge of Sun
To Steeple and to Rath,
To Mountain Church
And Fairy Fort,

A dual impetus
To rush the West
And lush embrace
Of soft-fleshed Pagan latitude,

Or narrow East
To inverse point of sharpened thorn;

'Till forced,
And then we rush
In post-to-ante pre-set faith
To hug the West, or bow to East
To touch the breast, or kiss the lips,
The leaven bread, the pagan feast,
To taste the flesh, to abjure the curse.

THE HILLS OF MY HOMELAND

From out the mist they are calling
The hills of my homeland,
Their purple heather beckoning
To their glens and braes again.
'Twas there in days of childhood
I walked beneath the sun
Where the bracken stored the moonlight
And the blossom tamed the whin.

O, to walk again my mountains
In the peace that I have known.
O, to lock again the secrets
Of my youth within the stone.

There shone a peace from Heaven
Where the bracken sped the rose
Round the winding lanes and pathways
That tiptoed round my home
And out along the hillsides
If with love and care you'd go
You'd hear the heart of Erin
Beating softly in the stone.
O, to walk again my mountains

In the peace that I have known.
O, to lock again the secrets
Of my youth within the stone.

But my hillsides long are ravished
And dark shadows crowd the stone
And the voice of pain now echoes
Through the bracken and the rose,
And the shadows gather daily
O'er those hilltops of the sun
And the roads that lead to heartache
Are the roads that we have run.

O, to walk again my mountains
In the peace that I have known.
O, to lock again the secrets
Of my youth within the stone.

Repeat Chorus.

THE CHAMPION'S PORTION

Fly high the flags of glory now
On new-dawn hills, unfurl the pride
In fifty years of hope long bound
As Macha wreathes at last her brow.

And to her list of kinsmen past
Who trod in fame Slieve Gullion's heights
Four names now add from out this time,
Henceforth they walk the heroes' path.

For Justin now and Enda sit
Amongst the host of Cumhal's men,
Defenders of our hopes and dreams,
To Macha's sons the fitting heirs.

And from Midh Luachra's furnace cast
Of anvil steel Mc Geeney came,
His courage as a time-beat lance,
In awe we watched him lead the fray.

Undaunted, proud, Mac Tiarnáin stood,
Fearless custodian of the line,
As stood Cuchulainn at the fjord,
No mightier his than Benny's hand.

And to these four is due this day
When in these hills sits Eire's prize,
And in this mythic place of dreams
On their heads we place our crown.

HE MASS ROCK
(18-6-2000)

A line of Policemen on duty,
Silent the bayonets and guns,
Protecting and guiding the pilgrims
Down pathways of crag and stone,
Through hedges and narrow passes,
Through fields where rhythms run
Of those who walked before us
In shelter of rock and whin
Down Penal paths long stealing
On this journey of their souls.

Music rising from hillsides
Rejoicing its public notes,
Bands playing a symphony
Long stored in faith and rock,
Beating the sound of advance
Loud on history's horn.

Words stealing a pathway
To the stone-patch where I write,
"In ainm an Athar agus an Mhic
Agus an Spioraid Naoimh —"
A timeless rhythm kinning,
Borne on the words of the priest,
Sound-stepping its origins
To the naked rock of our race,
Finding its way soft-footed
Into the rhyme of my verse.

The Mass rock here before me
On guard in shelter of hedge,
The figure of the cross engraved
Deep in its watching face.
The pilgrims pour their kindred,
One by one in its mould,
Raw lips on flesh of the stone.

I lay my hands upon it,
Warm from the heat of the sun,
And warm from the heat of ages,
Of those who laid their souls
Loyal in the vault of its stone.

God now being adored
In sparseness of hill and crag,
Disciples around in a circle,
A child adored in a stable
In bareness of rock and cradle,
Wise Men now announcing
The good news on mountain cable.

I faith myself in securely
Into this circle of ages.

BUILDING

Spade-poised on mound I stand
Beneath Slieve Gullion's brow
And dream again a dream of old
When men dug in the ground
And raised raw stone on bedrock laid
On centuries of toil
Who knew the tug and kiss of clay
The soft caress of soil.

I look up through this valley
Where poets walked of old,
Ó Doirnín and McCooey
Mc Alinden, Séamas Mór;
Brave sculptors of sweet melody
Who worked at the penal face
And carved their songs of beauty
On the history of our race.

As I look across these mountains
I feel their chisel edge,
Sheer as this edge of beauty,
Sharp flint at the heart's core.
And this will be my bedrock,
Here I place it now.
A cornerstone of hope I lay,
I seed it in the ground.

And I will wait till hawthorn blooms
Along these granite walls
And raise my head and chant a rune
As the dusk of twilight falls.
For I am back to rooted faith
Dug deep in hallowed ground
And raw impulses in the blood
That call to rock and stone.

HE HILL HEAD

The Crooked Road is silent now
The marching feet have passed,
Through bracken and through heather
They have walked him down to rest.

And silent now the empty house
Standing guard beneath the crag,
A mother's heart still beating there
Her whispered tears still round its hearth.

Beside the cradle there she'd sat
Her young man snatched from her side,
Ten strong sons, one daughter raised
On faith and tears and a mother's pride.

Long grown now the beaten tracks
Through Hill Head fields and neat-trimmed lanes,
One by one nine sons had passed,
One daughter left in foreign fields.

The last male heir he had watched alone
Through mirrored glass the slow decay
His worn face now holographed
On rising weeds and creeping fern.

And as the summer's sun gave way
To autumn haze on Mullion bog
He felt his own days closing in,
He knew too well the family path.

He would not walk these roads again
No others nurse, no new wreaths lay.
With death his lone companion now
He waited out his final days.

And from the trees that skirt the yard
A blackbird filled the autumn air,
Fit requiem from mountain ash
As they carried out his corpse.

The Hill-Head fields are silent now
Their hurried feet have passed
And silent now the aching walls
The sheltered lane and hearth.

THE WILD GEESE

Last night I saw the wild geese again
Shafting the sky at eve,
An arrow slung from a bow of time
Traversing forty years.

And I stood on the hill and watched them go
Winging their way to the south
And the wings they flapped were flapping in me
And their call was a distant voice.

And I heard again through the swish of years
From the headland where we'd sat
My father's tale when pipes were lit
The green hay at our backs.

A tale of men and foolish dreams
And an uncle, famed for schemes of wealth,
Who brought a hundred geese to roam
Across the hanging heath.

He watched with glee as they grew and grazed,
His fortunes surely made,
Until a distant Autumn day
When the wild geese passed again.

And his hundred geese, like a hundred dreams,
Rose on a single wing
And he watched his fortunes slowly fade
Across the southern whin.

My father smiled when his tale was done
And I raised my boyish head
And watched the wild geese wheel above
And wished I had wings as well.

To fly to the south with the wild geese then
Was the greatest dream I knew.
If I had wings last night I'd fly
Back through the withering years

And watch in awe as the wild geese veered
Across my father's words
And wing my way to each hallowed phrase
In a wild snow-down of tears.

ANNIVERSARIES

Where have you been while the flowers were dying,
Dew-crowned blossoms falling fast on stone,
Where rooted seed, pre-cast in soil of morning,
Their shoots now withered to a bleached ancestral bone?

Where were you when all the flowers were dying
That bloomed in soil that history's blade has turned,
When there walked men who sowed fresh hopes and visions
And "leaped to death" to grasp the chance you've won?

Speak not to me of love and stout endurance,
You who never learned to love your own
Whose minds are honed to preset edge of bias
That cuts its way through hope to win the Status Quo.

When again will we see flowers blooming
In craters deep which once were hearts of love
Whose hopes now lie like scattered seeds of yearning
Where flowering tombstones spread new blossoms on their pain?

Where will you be when the crops are blooming
That you plant now in soil long washed with tears?
And where will you be when young men are dying
To reap this harvest of your bitter years?

(Composed at the time of the first anniversary of the Omagh bombing/the retrieval of the first bodies of the "disappeared" from a bog/ and the Assembly cancellation.)

MORNING LIGHT
(A meeting between senior pupils
and delegated groups of first years)

Voices clutch at words of wisdom
In this rustling breeze of speech,
Faces turned with eyes of wonder
Towards their "Cara" as a source
Of the knowledge that they're seeking
Of the hidden way ahead,
Of the road where lie dark shadows
In the mist of unseen years.

In this morning light they're searching
For the key to unlock doors
From the savants who have turned them
In the padlock of their fears,
And who walk in rays of sunshine
Where the brightening path is clear
Where new light has banished darkness
And won knowledge points the way.

A PARENT'S BLESSING

The voice of spring is wafting now
Along the hills and valleys
And new flowers are speaking now
Of days of sun and laughter.

And I rejoice that you'll be there
With all your friends together
And new voices heard once more
Along the whispering rafters.

And may you find true peace within
That sanctuary of the mountains
And may the hands that guided Seers
Guide you down through the ages.

And in the evening as you sit
And gaze across the valley,
Be not afraid to weave your dreams
In gossamer of fancy.
And they will be like twinkling stars
In firmament of promise
As the drifting years roll slow
Across the hills eternal.

And soon the sun will shine again
Where bluebells paint the heather,
And soon the smile of hawthorn bloom
Will spread along the valley.

And may they be a bouquet brought
To you by hands of Angels,
And may they ever shine for you
And all your generations.

A MORNING PRAYER

God save me from the people
Who are wise,
Who seek the truth in shadows
And in clouds,
Who miss the obvious.

God save me from the people
Who dig deep,
Who strike inwards
For the pathway to the truth,
Who miss the obvious.

God save me from the pupils
Whom I teach,
Who daily shun simplicity
And seek
Deep mystery in my words,
Who miss the obvious.

CROWNS

From the sky they came,
Falling
Like the thorns of Christ
On the outstretched hands
Of the innocents,
Or a spear from a side,

And they piled
Cloud on cloud
Down the spiralled years
To the zero ground
Of that final day,

As might fall a cloud
Of piercing cries
From Hiroshima
Or prayers
Aimed at the hands of Christ
From torn mothers' hearts
Along the curved path
Of history's lasered course,

From denuded wastes
In Vietnam
And crucified heights
In Palestine
And blood-washed streets
In Tyrone.

In the East there hangs
High on history's cross
Another crown waiting
To be filled
For new infants of the cradle.

EVENING

I walk down the laneways of evening
Where the bright sun of morning once shone
And I see in the twilight still fleeting
The shadows we cast at the dawn.

I pause by the lane side and listen
To laughter that echoes far off
And I hear in the stillness low weeping
And I turn to find it's my heart.

I look back the laneway in wonder
Along the path we have come

But only shadows confront me,
Unseen now the pathways we trod.

And I wonder if others are walking
These laneways that stretch far behind
And I wonder if they too are thinking
The bright morning sun will not end.

For them a dark truth is now dawning
Behind the sharp rays of that sun
That will rise on the hilltops of evening
When the bright lanes of morning are run.

FAREWELL
(To my father – A debt owed)

I was afraid to say goodbye
Imprisoned there by your side,
Afraid that you would open eyes
To seek a truth to you denied.

Hung on every breath you made
Every move and every sigh
As nurses came and doctors pried
Hung on every twitch of eye.

You were too noble for deceit
Too true to basics in your life
As true as cut of sweeping scythe,
Not for you the readied lie.

The wide expanse of autumn fields
The harvest ripening in your veins
The steady grip of spade and plough,
Not for you harsh truth denied.

Your sacrifice so often made
Family first before your needs
No time for sickness or for pain
The force of duty driving on.

And now the time had come to pay
The debt of love that we all owed,
And I was lurking there in fear
Beneath the shadow of your pain.

And so you left without goodbye
Sliding into field and sky
Imprisoning me with peace denied,
Abandoned there by your side.

LANDSCAPE

I will not be at rest
The day you bury me.
Not for long days after,
'Till grass has grown
And flowers have taken root
And hawthorn leaves sweep low
On Molshy's height
Where summer lambs hug low
The shelter in the dappled shade.

Then seek me where the rabbits run,
Or in the dells where bluebells cluster,
Or on the heights
Where ditches rise to meet the sun,

And I'll be there
Where all our people are
Since time began,
Crowding close on hill and plain

In upland fields
And quarried lanes,

Whispering soft in lone wind-breaks
Where their dreams were laid.
A permanence of landscape,
Now they wait.

PATHWAYS

God walks in these hillsides
On pathways of white thorn
Where sunbeams kneel in homage
To kiss his outstretched hands
As he treads the haloed ridges
Of Slieve Gullion's peaks at dawn.

And in the fields of springtime
Where the loping vixen ran
To await the victor's coming
From the dew-crushed trampled fern
Through the throbbing high-arched meadow
To her whispering mountain lair.

And in the slanting stable
Beneath the crossbeam cracked
Where the fresh-downed trembling hollow
In the darkened mud-pie lashed
Spoke of swallows late returned there,
New-winged into the night.

And in the mountain churchyard
Where the bell its three notes spoke
To announce my father's coming
To the arms we faithed were stretched
From beyond the twilight shadows
To embrace him in the dark.

SACRIFICE

If I could pen forty years
Into the corral of one word
And lay it before God,
White-skinned, chalk-pured,
On the altar of my days,
Would I win forgiveness
For my life's neglect,

For the thoughts not stored
Deep in vaulted words
And I on bended knee
Throughout my days
Instead of trying now
To clear the debt
In the twilight of my words?

SHADOWS

When you first stepped out alone
Down the staring aisle
I saw her shadow by your side
As her coffin passed me by.

Did she guide your footsteps then
On that lonely course
Down a path so long un-trod
Towards a world so long unknown?

Severed now, you paced her slow,
Your eyes adrift to where she'd sat
The aching void now part of you,
A present, outer, self.

Beside the open door you paused
Then stepped into the light
Its cutting edge as sharp as steel
Honed to a shock of truth.

No plaintiff cry that I have heard
Across Slieve Gullion's peaks
Could match the pain within your eyes
The scream of silence from your heart.

And now you walk the Milltown road
Plucking echoes from the wind,
Her voice now silent in the fields
Her laughter dying in the hills.

THE TADPOLE AND THE FROG
(A Satire)

"I am wise," the fat frog said,
"I rule with power and might.
I squat upon this pond all day
And I think throughout the night."

The tadpole looked at him with awe
And marvelled at his size,
His jowelled cheeks, his bulging head,
The wisdom in his eyes.

"I am weak," the tadpole said,
"I'm not like you at all.
I have no legs, my head is small
And I've got this tail as well."

"Just follow me," the fat frog said.
"I'll teach you wonders new,
All the things that you must know
So one day you may rule."

"How can I rule?" the tadpole asked
And swam up to his side,
"I have no brain, I'm not like you,
You are so strong and wise!"

"You're learning fast!" the fat frog croaked
And laid a minnow low,
"To praise the strong is to be wise,
To flatter and cajole."

"And are there other things to learn?"
The tadpole asked and jumped
Into the fat frog's arms and stroked
His long tail on his cheek.

"You are too young," the fat frog said,
"All knowledge to impart.
There is a truth, a secret deep,
That those who rule must learn."

The fat frog leaped into the pond,
He made a mighty splash.
The tadpole followed close behind,
He followed day and night.

He watched the tricks the fat frog used
To rule and terrorise.
He saw the minnows bow to him.
He watched them cringe with fright.

But though he noted all the tricks
And was so keen to learn,
That hidden truth eluded him.
He felt now deep despair.

Each day he searched inside his head
But still no brain could find.
"I'll never rule!" the tadpole wailed.
"I never will be wise."

One morning when the tadpole woke
He gave a mighty shout.
Four legs had grown, his tail was gone
And his head was large and stout.

He rushed into the pond and sought
The fat frog in the reeds.
"I am just like you!" he cried,
"And ready now to rule."

"And have you found that truth?" he asked,
 And gulped an errant fry,
"That secret deep that you must know
To rule the meek and mild?"

"That truth I've got," the tadpole croaked,
"It came with my large head.
 For us to rule and terrorise
 We need no brain at all!"

The two frogs sat together now
The minnows gathered round.
They gazed at them with awe and thought,
"They look so very wise!"

UNDERCURRENT

It is the voice of man I hear,
The voice of loneliness, of fear,
Calling from hills and sunlit plains
From crowded streets

From silent lanes,
Hushed in the grass that waves
On spring-filled days
In song of birds
In mountain streams;

A voice that speaks
Of you and me
Of distant lands
Of crowded seas,
A voice that speaks
Of ways and days
Of sliding hours
Of silent graves.

WILL YOU?

Will you come along with me
Across the hillsides wide
To where the honeybee
Sips nectar from the flowers?

Will you come along with me
To where the hawthorn blooms
In valleys burning red
In the berry-ripening noon?

Will you walk with me a while
Where mountain rivers run
And dewdrops kiss the daisies
Asleep amidst the fern?

Will you walk with me a while
In the evening's silken calm
To where the deep lough waters
Catch stars within their arms?

And will you sit with me and wonder
For a moment of your day
At the hand that plucked this beauty
From dead and barren clay?

And will you raise your head and whisper
To the mighty and the proud
To close their tomes of wisdom
And read the script before their eyes?

CELEBRATING
(Silver Jubilee of Lislea Drama Festival)

This festival of faith begun
By savants of the ancient stage
Rekindled sparks still smouldering
Within the embers of the years
And past and present met once more
Upon this schoolhouse stage.
From north and south we watched them come
To tread these boards and savour still
The mystic paths that words can weave
To hidden regions of the heart.
And crowds flocked in to pack this hall,
Vying often for a place
On winter nights of cold and frost
To sit again on creaking chairs
And beat in tune with living words.

The setting changed, the purpose still
The celebration of ourselves,
Of rural values and of truth,
Of friendship and of céilí house.
And so it was and still remains
A quarter of a century thence,
The five and twenty gilded years
Since Ownie's dream was realised.

And bright-eyed youths now walk this stage
As yet unborn when we began,
And they in turn new rhythms weave
For those who sit unseen in awe,
Bestowing man's most precious gift
The memories stored in childhood hearts.

Tonight we meet to celebrate
The wonder of these newfound years
When dreams of faith and hope came true,
So may it be in future days.
And when the clock rolls on again
A quarter of a century hence
May we be heard in rhythmic words
Dancing live upon this stage.

THE LONG HILL

Humped-back temptress of his days,
Refusing to accept your infertility
He straddled your height each year
And fathered your wizened crop
Of weeds,

Flaunting your promise
As the sharp plough unzipped your earth
Encouraging his rape
Until the weakness of years brought impotence
And he ignored your call.

I too felt the urge
To rummage your cold frigidity
When effort was expendable
In the wild largess of youth. Now
I only sit and follow the slow track
Of his feet up your eternal slope

And see that unwittingly
He ravaged your proud contempt.
His seed breeds strong his memory
Deep-rooted in your veins and yields
His form with every turn of eye.

I harvest him
Each time his autumn calls.

PRISTINE FORMS

There is no Celtic twilight here. These
Men walk in sun. Their flashing
Fire burns sweet incense of another day.
I looked through the vacant eye of
Calmor's cave, drawn inwards as the shadows
Clawed their clammy fist down my
Spinal cord, answering in childhood
The legend's call unknowing.
Later the truth dawned. The name released its
Secret and Cathal Mór walked down,
Highwayman of culture, who dragged me
Through the eye to touch his hidden store
Of high-jacked years. Now they walk
From veils of shadows into the baying
Mouth of dawn. There walks

Finn McCool and Oisín flung
In that man's form enacting his saga
Of fields and Niamh walks the country road
Radiant in simplicity. They stir
An echo from bed of hills warm
From centuries of slumber, the mind
Plays their tune recorded in contoured
Fields and sleep-dimmed eyes, as real now
In their rephrase.

That deep-faced man
Sits by the lake's edge consumed by sheep
And heather-bloom unaware he is pursued
By battalions of years. The deep lough waters
Sit awaiting his leap. Only in this
Is he known. He will pass the baton
On, future generations clamor
At the mark.

How else can they be called?
Unreal as this lung of fields
And chanting roads in modern interpretation.
No Freudian phrase will analyze, no
Social term encompass them. They walk
A hidden line within themselves stretching
Back a thousand years unaware they mime
A pristine form.

I lie beside them
In this bed of hills and snuggle close
To their warmth of years.

THE INHERITOR
(From the old Irish)

He loped his way through his newfound land,
The laziest man around,
Until he reached the widow's patch
And he raised his head in the wind.

He loped his way to the garden wall
And measured it out in his mind,
A hundred feet to the angled patch
Give or take a thousand pounds.

And he loped his way through the points in law
And found she was eighty five
Bound to the chair with a cripple's stick
And he smiled as he did her down.

MY SON

I pray to the son you killed,
You hanged him from a tree,
He whose heart was full
Of love for you and me.

I watched you die, my son,
A mother's tears I shed.
I watched your love still shine
Even in your pain.

I cradled you, my son,
As child and infant born.
I cradled you, my son,
When your flesh from the tree was torn.

The evil that men do
You gave your life to atone,
The evil that men do
Your death, my beloved son.

Eternal now my pride
As I see your victory won,
Eternal now your throne,
My sweet Jesus, my son.

THE DANCE

She stood on the floor beside them
When the music's strains had died
And thought of the years that ground them
And the years before her now.

For soon, by the light of dawning,
Before their tears had dried
She'd be off to the train and the moorings
And the ship of a thousand sighs.

And she knew that their hearts were breaking
Beneath their bright gay smiles
And she played their own game bravely
As she skipped to the final tune.

Then round by the Bainseach laneway
And down by the Cargan stile
Through paths of youth and laughter
Slow-paced they led her now.

And children stepped beside her,
Those waiting next in line,
As they walked her in the mist of the morning
On the first of her emigrant miles.

And they crowded the height and waved her
As the carriage bore her on
round by the rocks of "Birget
And down by the Cailleach's lane.

And she watched as they slowly faded
Into the greying mists of dawn
And she left her heart there with them
Locked deep in those hills of pain.

NATIVE PATHS

He fell in love with words
Early in his life
As he ran the hills,
Along time-worn paths
Where rhythms beat from rock
Of language turned to stone,
Congealed to hill and crag
When history sought the heights,
Along time's margin laid
Like glosses where he walked;
Aughanduff, Ballard, Lislea,
Slievebreak, Burr, Croslieve.

And they called to him
In rhythm's bondage locked,
De-petrified on tongue
To lilting native paths,
Through language of landscape.

And to his mind was born
Twin progeny of verse,
The one his father's voice
Kithed to him at birth,
The other kinned him out
To the Gap of North,
And tongued in stones their voice
By Moyry's ancient pass
As he turned a key
In history's stiffened lock
And saw through dawning light,
Close by, his ancestry.

FINAL CHORUS

Now around this ring of Gullion
A silence falls on voices
That we knew
And tombstones point to darkening corners
Where low shadows crowd
Across the bray,
Where grass is greener now
For love and pity,
A blush of green where walls
And windows stood.
The cows graze on their dreams
And tramp their visions in
And wander heedless
Through their crowded years.

The empty corners echo hurried footsteps
And hands that lurked in ambush
On decay
And faces bright with friendship
At the doorway,
The table spread with poverty's
Full array.
The two-pronged daughin marks
The beaten hearthstone
Where plans were made
And far-off dreams were laid
And aching limbs were quenched
In liquid twilight,
Their minds afloat on tides
Of passing day.
But we are left, the guardians
Of their treasures
To reap the harvest of
Their planted dreams

And answer echoes from
Across these hillsides
Of voices low that whisper
In our veins.
And we but raise that voice
In final chorus
To plant a tongue in grass
That grows unseen
Where hurried feet once beat a
Troubled pathway
Towards the crowded corners
Where we dwell.